Frances Kidder
The Last Woman Publicly Hanged in England

Runic Productions
01233 713104

to Stwuff

Frances Kidder

The Last Woman Publicly Hanged in England

James Nicholls

ERIC DOBBY PUBLISHING

First published 2010 by

Eric Dobby Publishing Ltd
Random Acres
Slip Mill Lane
Hawkhurst
Cranbrook
Kent TN18 5AD

Disclaimer
Every effort has been made to trace the owners of copyright material used in this book; should any material have been included inadvertently without the permission of the owner of the copyright, acknowledgment will be made in any future edition.

ISBN 978-1-85882-067-5

Printed in India by Replika Press

Cover design by Insignia Graphics Ltd

Contents

Illustrations

James Nicholls

James Nicholls was born in Sidcup, Kent and educated at the Hurstmere School for Boys, Sidcup and at colleges in the City of London and Holborn where he studied law, economics and political history. In the1960s he was a broker at Lloyds of London where he specialized in legal liability insurance in the construction industry. Instead of pursuing an expected career in law, in the early 1970s he became a contractual liability insurance specialist for a major construction and engineering group before returning to the City. Throughout the 1980s and 1990s he was an independent insurance and financial adviser.

For many years he has studied English mediaeval history and a special interest has been the 14th century, including Edward The Black Prince and his son, Richard II. As a criminal law historian, James has extensively studied the cases of Bentley-Craig (1952), James Hanratty and the A6 Murder (1961), Ruth Ellis (1955), the Guildford Four and the Birmingham Six. James believes that if a referendum on the return of capital punishment was held today the majority of people would vote in its favour. However, many miscarriages of justice have convinced him that we cannot accept the return of capital punishment if our criminal justice system can fail with disconcerting frequency.

Among his many other interests are the environment, politics, and British wildlife. A committed exponent and devotee of satire, James also wrote comedy scripts for television and radio in the 1980s.

He lives in an eighteenth-century cottage on the North Downs in Kent and has had articles and booklets published on the Pilgrims Way, the ancient track from Winchester to Canterbury. His other published works include articles on: *The Medway Megaliths*, *Ratty: A Sad Tale Of The Riverbank* (the plight of the water vole), *Joan of Kent*, *Hawkinge Fighter Base*, *The Witches of Kent*, and *Thomas Becket – Saint or Sinner?*

Preface

My interest in criminal law history, especially local cases, began many years ago in the late 60s and early 70s when I was studying law in London. I discovered the case of Frances Kidder, "the wicked stepmother", a few years ago when I was researching an article on "The Witches of Kent". Her crime had generated such hatred and disgust that many local Romney Marsh people had accused her of witchcraft and of summoning the Devil through the spirit of the dead Louisa, the poor girl she had drowned in a ditch near New Romney. Certainly, if the local people had managed to wrest Frances from the arms of the law, they would have hanged her from a suitable tree or a pitchfork would have been plunged into her neck; this being the manner in which the mob dealt with accused witches in mid-seventeenth century England and Frances might well have suffered the same fate 200 years later.

But Frances Kidder was not a witch – she was a cold-blooded murderess and the law of nineteenth-century England dealt with her accordingly.

For many years I have also studied the case of Ruth Ellis, the last woman hanged in Britain. My interest in the case was enhanced when I learned that, as a young boy in 1954, I sat on Ruth's lap in my aunt's house in St Paul's Cray, Kent. Apparently, on one occasion, Ruth also took me to buy sweets at the local shops. My aunt – my mother's sister – was the friend and neighbour of

Muriel, Ruth's older sister. Ruth often visited Muriel, sometimes with Desmond Cussen, another man in her life at that time. Ruth Ellis had just lost her baby – through a miscarriage or otherwise – and was out of her mind on Pernod and the tranquillizer Librium, to which she was addicted, when she pumped four bullets into her lover, David Blakely, outside the *Magdala* public house in Tanza Road, Hampstead in the evening of Easter Sunday, the 10th of April 1955. In Holloway Prison, at 9am on Wednesday morning the 13th of July 1955, Ruth Ellis made criminal history as the last woman hanged in Britain. As a result of the Ruth Ellis case the 'defence' (or mitigation) of Diminished Responsibility was enshrined in the Homicide Act of 1957 and allowed those charged with murder to have the charge reduced to manslaughter on the grounds that the accused was not fully responsible for his or her actions at the time of the murder.

At noon on Thursday, the 2nd of April 1868, outside Maidstone Prison, Frances Kidder became the last woman hanged in full public view for the murder of her eleven-year-old step-daughter, Louisa Kidder-Staples. Nearly two months later, on May the 29th 1868, the Capital Punishment (Within Prison Amendment) Act was passed and thereafter the general public could not witness the ghastly sight of a person struggling at the end of a rope in the name of justice. This small step on the grinding treadmill of the British criminal justice system would lead to the abolition of the death penalty 100 years later.

Ruth Ellis did not deserve to hang, Frances Kidder did. Ruth Ellis died instantly at the hands of her executioner, Frances Kidder did not. Both Ruth Ellis and Frances Kidder had little defence available to them other than to prove they were "temporarily insane", as described in the M'Naghten Rules of 1843, but in both cases this defence was not run. In Ruth Ellis's case it might have been successful; in Frances Kidder's case it would not have been. Ruth Ellis elicited an enormous amount of public sympathy before and after her execution; public sympathy for Frances Kidder was voiced only after she had been executed.

Just 87 years separated the two women who made historic landmarks in the criminal justice system of our country. Subject to the discipline of the nineteenth-century criminal justice regime in which Frances Kidder was convicted, her execution could not be regarded as a miscarriage of justice. Within the structure and interpretation of the twentieth-century Homicide Act, which compelled trial judge Justice Havers to sentence Ruth Ellis to death, her execution could not be regarded as a miscarriage of justice either, although there was a serious absence of judicial prudence, which could have been exercised by the Home Secretary, Major Gwilym Lloyd George.

Lloyd George had the power to reprieve her but he chose not to do so. One of the reasons, it has been suggested, was that had Ruth Ellis's sentence of death been commuted to life imprisonment this would have "opened the floodgates" to a legion of frustrated, miserable, and grieved wives and mistresses to murder their boring, unfaithful, violent, and cruel husbands and lovers without compunction or fear of the ultimate penalty.

Frances Kidder could not appeal because there was no appeal system and her trial judge did not consider her case worthy of a recommendation for a commutation of sentence. Both Ellis and Kidder were rightfully convicted of their crimes and both were rightly punished by their respective criminal justice systems: in 1955 Justice Havers had no choice under the prevailing Homicide Act and Justice Byles had no choice under the prevailing criminal law in 1868.

Many criminal historians maintain that Ruth Ellis had an accomplice when she killed David Blakely in the evening of that fateful Easter Sunday in 1955: the person who supplied her with the gun, whoever that may have been. But however Ruth obtained the gun, when she pointed it at Blakely, did she not intend to kill him? When asked this question by prosecution counsel, Christmas Humphreys, in the Number 1 Court of the Old Bailey, she simply replied: "Of course I did". Frances Kidder did not have an accomplice: she intentionally killed her step-daughter with her own hands and in her own time, and for that she paid the ultimate penalty. Both women were proven to have intended the inevitable consequences of their actions; both women were dealt with by the criminal justice system of their times.

However, this tragic story takes us back to mid-nineteenth-century Victorian England, when the administration of justice was comparatively cheap, when there was no legal aid, and when it was possible to be flogged and sentenced to hard labour or transported to the Australian penal colonies for the offence of financial irresponsibility and recklessness with other people's money entrusted to you. The recent horrors of the "Credit Crunch" – together with the names of not a few bankers – comes to mind here and personally I would not find the nineteenth-century punishment meted out to these people at all disagreeable.

But our sorry tale concerns a potato salesman from Hythe, the daughter of an agricultural labourer from New Romney, and an innocent child.

I do hope you find it interesting.

James Nicholls
The North Downs, Kent
July 2010

Introduction

The young woman sat quietly on a large box in her parents' bedroom of the small farm-worker's cottage in New Romney. She stared fixedly at the floor, a look of sullen defiance on her attractive face. She had changed into fresh, dry clothes: a smart dark linen dress and tight, black laced boots. Her other clothes, which included a soaking wet and muddy light spotted dress, had been hurriedly thrown under the bed.

It was just after 10 o'clock on a Sunday evening in the late summer of 1867 and the annual town fair had come to an end. It had been a warm day but now there was a welcome freshness in the air and the dew began to settle in the soft, mellow fields of Romney Marsh as the townsfolk, chattering and laughing, made their way home. But in the bedroom of the small cottage there was only tension, anger and anxiety.

The young woman's husband, a man 14 years her senior, had arrived at her parents' cottage a little over half an hour earlier. He had expected to collect her, their daughter Emma, who was nearly 3 years old, and Louisa, his 11 year-old daughter from a previous relationship. He had expected to take them back home to Hythe in his pony and trap. But the young woman had taken Louisa out earlier that evening and had returned to the cottage without her. Now, her husband William and her parents demanded to know where Louisa was. She had told them that Louisa had been frightened by some horses and had fallen into a ditch. But they had not believed her. They had good reason not to believe her. That's why they had summoned the local police officer, Benjamin Aspinall. Because she would not tell them where Louisa was. Because they feared the worst.

"What will you have me do with your wife, Kidder ?", Aspinall had asked firmly.

At William's request his young wife was arrested and taken in William's pony and trap to the town hall lock-up a few hundred yards away. As she climbed down from the little trap 24-year-old Frances Kidder, suddenly spitting with rage and eyes blazing with fury, cursed her husband and struck him violently. Then her face and her voice softened as she turned to the policeman and whispered: "You will find her at Mr Cobb's bridge."

Chapter 1

Origins

In the mid-nineteenth century New Romney was a bustling Kent town that enjoyed the prestigious status of "Cinque Port". It was once possessed of a harbour and the town grew rich on the business brought in by the trading ships and barges.

The splendid twelfth century Norman parish church of St Nicholas was founded by William The Conqueror's half-brother, Bishop Odo the Earl of Kent, in AD 1086 the year of the Domesday Book, in which Romney is recorded as "Romenel". The town's name is derived from the Saxon/Early English: "Rumen-ea", which translates as "(broad) marsh water".

In 8th-century Kent the inhabitants of Romney Marsh were known as the "Merscewarre", from the Old English meaning: "(the) dwellers in the marsh".

In the mid-thirteenth century the mouth of the River Rother was a vast expanse of water between New Romney and Lydd and to the west the Cinque Ports of Rye and Winchelsea were situated in what was effectively a large sea "lake", surrounded by a shingle bank. However from 1250 a series of violent storms destroyed the shingle and with it the ports of New Romney and Winchelsea. Consequently, Winchelsea had to relocate to higher ground where it stands today and New Romney lost its port.

During the fifteenth century a drainage and sea defence system was installed which continued up until the mid-16th century. But throughout the eighteenth century this drainage system required more people than were available to manage it and it suffered accordingly. The poor management of the dykes and channels led to stagnation in many areas and this bred marsh mosquitos, which were responsible for outbreaks of malaria and for many deaths in and around the Marsh, including New Romney and Lydd. However as the drainage system was enlarged and improved this dreadful disease receded and the reclaimed land was ideal for root and cereal crops. The Romney sheep industry expanded rapidly at this time and the renowned "Romney" was exported to the colonies of Australia, New Zealand and also Van Diemens Land (Tasmania). The construction, in 1806, of the 28 mile Royal Military Canal from Hythe to Cliff End, near Rye, to repel Napoleon, greatly assisted the drainage of Romney Marsh. The Canal, which fortunately Napoleon never saw, was completed in April 1809, together with the famed Martello Towers. A total of 74 towers were built, the last being at Seaford in East Sussex.

From the seventeenth to the late nineteenth centuries, smuggling was a highly profitable industry, with the Marsh being a favoured haunt and hiding place of these nefarious scoundrels. Smuggling was not only concerned with the illegal importation of tobacco and spirits; wool and livestock (sheep) were also exported by Marsh smugglers to their counterparts in France. Two of the most infamous gangs were the Owlers (because they made "hooting" sounds as secret signals) and the Aldington gang, also known as the "Blues" and run mainly by the notorious Ransley family from their 'headquarters' at The Walnut Tree pub in that delightful Kent village on the edge of Romney Marsh. Two of the Ransley brothers, William and James, convicted of burglary and hanged at Penenden Heath on the 24th of August 1800, are buried in the churchyard of St Mary Magdalene at Ruckinge. They were hanged along with their accomplice, Isaac Ballard, the innkeeper of *The Blue Anchor*, the mid-eighteenth century inn at Ruckinge, another meeting place of the smugglers.

Such was New Romney's political and commercial importance that, from 1371, the town sent two members of parliament (or "Barons") to the Commons at every election until it was abolished as a borough and a constituency in 1832 under the Reform Act; the town was incorporated in the new East Kent Division. Up until the reform of 1832, New Romney was termed a "rotten borough", mainly because the influence of a few major landowning families determined who was elected.

A Charter of Incorporation had been granted in the mid-fourteenth century by Edward III, who issued market charters to many Kent towns and villages in order to earn taxes (wool "staples") for his wars against the French. A new Charter was granted by Elizabeth I in 1562, confirming the town's status as a Cinque Port and instituting a mayor and 'jurats', and in 1885 Queen Victoria issued another Charter, which gave New Romney a mayor, four aldermen, and twelve councillors under the 1882 Municipal Corporations Act. A gas station was constructed in 1854 and New Romney High Street was street-lighted in the same year.

Romney Marsh was and is renowned for being one of the most productive agricultural areas in Europe and, after the Romans initially drained it nearly 2000 years ago, what was once the sea bed of the English Channel is now a rich, fertile soil ideal for potatoes and other root vegetables and cereal crops. In the mid-nineteenth century those farmers and landowners fortunate enough to have the money and the skills to exploit this agricultural King Solomon's Mines became rich and prospered in lean times when others went wanting. Merchants, and general dealers in vegetable crops, made a good living out of the Marsh, and its inhabitants – many of whom laboured tirelessly on the land – made their own often meagre living from the precious soil.

Kidder, Staples and Turner
The Kidder Family

One such general dealer was William Kidder who was born in 1828 in Saltwood or Lyminge (Etchinghill), near Hythe. His parents were George Kidder, a baker, and Mary (nee Down) who were married at St Mary's church, Sellindge on the 18th of October 1825. In the Hythe Parish Records of 1828 William Henry Kidder is recorded as baptised on the 7th of November and his brother, Edmund George Kidder, was also baptised on the same day.

In the 1841 Census for Lyminge the family is recorded as living at Etchinghill and William is shown, aged 13, together with his mother Mary, aged 37. A 15-year-old brother George (this may have been "Edmund") is mentioned as is sister Bertha, who is aged 10 at this time. Father George is not recorded and it is possible that he was deceased.

In the mid-nineteenth century the Kidder family appears to be widespread throughout Kent, especially in the Wye, Sellindge and Hythe areas. The name may be Saxon in origin: an early translation of "Kydder" means "a hawker" or "travelling trader", and the name "Kyddere" appears in a land deed during the reign of Edward II, in the early-fourteenth century. Ironically, this information comes from a history compiled in 1850 by the Rector of Maresfield, the Reverend Edward Turner: another Turner with which a Kidder would be associated. In the seventeenth century a large Kidder family is found in East Sussex, especially East Grinstead and Maresfield, and from where, it appears, many members emigrated to the New World of America.

There are records of a Kidder family in Cranbrook in the 1630s and, in the Kent Poll Book of 1790, a George Kidder owns property in "Chidingstone" (Chiddingstone near Hever and Penshurst). There is another family of Kidders in and around Godmersham, near Wye, in the late-seventeenth century, and in the published Wills of 1853 we find a Thomas Kidder, yeoman of the parish of Hastingleigh near Wye, who died that year on the 11th April, leaving his estate to his wife, Susanna, and daughter, Elizabeth. In the parish census of 1871 a 70-year-old Thomas Kidder, a farm labourer, is living in Chartham, near Canterbury. However, in the Bridge Union Workhouse record, dated 1881, an 80 year-old "pauper inmate" named Thomas Kidder is recorded. If this is the same man he had clearly fallen on hard times as so many poor farm workers did when their labouring skills were replaced by farm machinery. It is assumed that these people were all members of the Kidder family in this part of Kent throughout the nineteenth century.

In 1861 William Kidder lived with Eliza Staples and their 4-year-old child, Louisa, in Theatre Street, off the High Street in Hythe, and he traded in the town, in Dymchurch, and around the Romney Marsh area. Various vocational descriptions of him are: "greengrocer", "carrier" and "huckster", a title that often applied to a hawker or door-to-door salesman. In the *Kelly's Directory* of 1862 he is described as a "saddler". William and Eliza had been in a relationship for several years and in early 1863 their second child Ellen was born. But both Louisa and Ellen were illegitimate because the couple had not married. Not unnaturally this had caused frequent problems between them, not least because nineteenth century Hythe did not encourage unmarried mothers in what was then a straight-laced and popular Victorian seaside holiday resort for the higher income middle class. Furthermore, William was not one to rush into marriage, as we shall see. However, Eliza seems determined to have afforded her children some degree of respectability because both children are recorded in the Hythe Parish Records as being baptised on the 8th of February 1863, soon after the birth of Ellen. At this time Louisa would have been 6 years of age as she was born in Hythe (St Leonard) on the 13th of November 1856. Although William is Ellen's father, both children are registered baptised as the daughters of "Eliza Staples"; William Kidder is not mentioned in the record and Louisa's birth registration states Eliza Staples as the mother but there is no record of the father. This may have been a simple error by the registrar or, significantly, Louisa's father was not William Kidder. However, in the later records, both children have the surname "Kidder-Staples".

Eliza's name is mentioned as "Sarah" once or twice in the later local newspaper reports but her name, on all of the records, is "Eliza" and it is by this name that she should be known. She had a younger sister, Sarah, who was born in 1848, and the local press may have confused the two girls: in 1861 Sarah would have been only 13. Sarah died in late September 1883, aged 37, and she was buried on the 2nd of October 1883.

The Staples Family

Eliza Staples was born in 1837 in Hothfield (Hothfield Street) near Ashford, Kent. Her father, Richard Staples, was also born in Hothfield in 1813 and in the 1841 Hothfield Census there is also a woman by the name of Staples who is aged 65; this is possibly Richard's paternal grandmother. In the 1851 Hothfield Census a six-year-old Celia Staples is recorded as blind and living in Hothfield with a family of Tappenden; it is not known if Celia is Eliza's sister but she is certainly a near relative. Eliza appears to have moved from Hothfield at an early age because, in 1841, we find a five-year-old Eliza Staples living in the household of Mr Henry and Mrs Sarah Clifford in the Ashford "suburb" of Kennington, the reason for which is not clear. Sarah Clifford is the mother of Richard Staples and is therefore Eliza's paternal grandmother. However by 1851 Eliza is recorded as aged 14 and living in Sellindge with her family. We do not know when Eliza met William or when they moved to Hythe but as Louisa was born in mid-November 1856, Eliza would have conceived in February of 1856 and it is quite possible that she was ordered out of the house if no wedding was planned; later events would suggest that Richard Staples thought his daughter had married William soon after. However if William was not the father of Louisa, he may have offered to live with 20 year-old Eliza and her child and they may have moved to Hythe just before Louisa was born in November of 1856; at this time William was aged 28 years.

In the 1871 Census for Sellindge we find 56-year-old Richard Staples (he is in fact 58) married to 55 year-old Rebecca and living with their five children and Richard's 76-year-old widowed mother, Mrs Sarah Clifford. William and Eliza's child, the eight-year-old Ellen Kidder-Staples, is also living with the family. Richard and Rebecca had a total of eight children and he worked for the South Eastern Railway as a plate-layer; in the records Richard is described as a "railway labourer" (the railway reached Ashford in December of 1842). Richard Staples was buried on the 11th March 1889, aged 77. He survived Rebecca by six and a half years; she was buried on 5th October 1883, aged 67.

Although he was not a rich man William Kidder made a reasonably comfortable living, as did most self-employed general dealers and traders in the 1860s. But with a domestic situation that offered little but seemingly interminable problems, not least because of his apparent reluctance to enter into matrimony, and with his work taking him away from home, William sought comfort elsewhere. It was no surprise therefore that on his frequent visits to New Romney, where he dealt with his suppliers, he met a local girl called Frances Turner who was 14 years his junior and the daughter of John Turner, a farm labourer, and his wife, also named Frances.

The Turner Family of New Romney

John and Frances Turner and their many children lived in a rented farm worker's cottage on the Dymchurch Road, outside New Romney. Of the eleven recorded children, nine were girls with Frances being the eldest. The Turners were not desperately poor but with such a large family to feed they would not have been financially comfortable. John Turner was a self-employed agricultural labourer and his wife may also have been a farm worker or a serving-woman in and around the increasingly prosperous ancient Cinque Port town. In 1865 the average weekly wage for an agricultural labourer was 11 shillings *(Schedules of Income 1860 to 1865)*.

During his visits to New Romney, William would have seen or met Frances who appears to have been something of a "free spirit", a nineteenth century version of a town "ladette". She would have mixed freely with "out-of-towners", as anyone living outside a radius of five miles of New Romney was known, and it is likely that William would have made the acquaintance of Frances's father, John, through his connections with the farm-working community in and around New Romney. It is equally likely that Frances would have returned William's wink and a smile on more than one occasion and one day perhaps he decided to chance his luck. Frances was young, attractive – seemingly a bit wild – and out for a good time and probably looking for an escape from the mediocrity of her dull, often pointless, existence. To Frances, anyone not tied to the land in a relentless daily grind of agricultural labouring would have been a "businessman" and thus she probably thought William was not short of a Queen's shilling either.

In the National Census of 1861 (dated the 7th of April) the Turner family of Dymchurch Road, New Romney is listed as follows:

John, aged 44, agricultural labourer, born in Ashford circa 1817;
his wife Frances, aged 35, born in Brenchley circa 1826.
The children are listed as:
Mary, aged 13 (baptised 6th February 1848),
Adelaide, aged 11 (baptised 2nd June 1850),
Rhoda, aged 5 (baptised 30th December 1855),

Harriet, aged 3 (baptised 20th September 1857),
Naomi, aged 1 (baptised 15th January 1860),
John James, aged 6 weeks (baptised 14th April 1861).
There are three children missing from the list:
Emma, baptised 24th November 1844, aged circa 17,
Ruth, baptised 15th March 1846, aged circa 15,
Frances, aged 18 or 19.
NB: The Turners produced two more children after 1861:
Charles Robert, baptised 29th March 1864 and Agnes, baptised
1st December 1867.

In the mid-nineteenth century, it was a serious offence to omit or
provide misleading information on a National Census, sometimes
punishable by imprisonment. Since the first Census, in 1801,
successive governments were anxious to maintain a strict
record of the population of the country and the movement of its
citizens; not least for taxation purposes, housing requirements,
and the surveillance and pursuit of the criminal classes. When
the first Census was finally completed government officials were
astonished to discover the population of England and Wales was
8.9 million and Scotland was 1.6 million. The figure for Ireland
was estimated as circa 5 million and in the Census of 1831 it
was confirmed as 7.7 million. At the end of the 18th century, the
unofficial estimates were between 6 and 7 million for England
and Wales but there were no reliable estimates for Scotland or
Ireland *(National Statistics)*. The punishment for refusing to
comply with or failing to comply with a Census request in the
mid-nineteenth century was a large fine or possible imprisonment
and in view of John Turner's strict adherence to the letter of the
law, which we shall see later, it seems likely that Emma, Ruth,
and Frances were working away from home in 1861. However,
Frances is recorded in the Census of 1851, aged eight years,
where she is described as "a scholar".

In 1861, we find that the Turner's next-door neighbours are also
a family of Turners as follows:

William Turner (head of household) is also an agricultural labourer, and aged 44 – the same age as John. However, William's birthplace is stated as New Romney, whereas John's is stated as Ashford, so it is possible that they were cousins; it seems inconceivable that they were not related in some way.

William's wife is 31 year-old Ann, who was born in Wye. Their daughters are listed as:

Charlotte, aged 2 (baptised on 13th June 1858),

Mary Ann, aged 1,

and, curiously, Elizabeth "Austen" is recorded as their 9 year-old daughter who was also born in Wye.

It is not clear when John Turner moved from his home town of Ashford to New Romney but, in the 1841 New Romney Census, his family members are recorded thus:

John Turner, agricultural labourer, aged 70 – this is probably John's grandfather because in the same house are:

James Turner, agricultural labourer, aged 45 – John's father, and:

John Turner, agricultural labourer, aged 25 – born circa 1817.

At another address is another John Turner, aged 45 and a labourer, and his wife, Mary, aged 40. They have at least six children but it is not clear if these Turners are related because "William", John's next door neighbour in 1861, is not mentioned as a child of this couple.

Frances Turner (Kidder) – Born in Brenchley, Kent

In the later press reports of 1868 Frances is stated as aged 25 years and in the 1851 Census for New Romney she is recorded as eight years old and living at New Romney as the daughter of John and Frances Turner. Therefore, it has been assumed that she was born in New Romney in 1843. However, although there is no record of a Frances Turner born or baptized in New Romney in 1843, the 1851 New Romney Census shows that both her mother Frances and Frances herself were born in the Brenchley area, near Tonbridge.

After a lengthy investigation of the records for Brenchley, Frances Turner's reported birth date must be revised.

The only birth certificate for a Frances being born the daughter of a Frances in Brenchley in 1843 is for Frances Frith, daughter of Samuel Frith and his wife Frances Frith – "formerly Neal". The birth date is the 18th of December 1843 and the birth is registered on the 12th of January 1844. This Frances is registered as baptized on the 21st of January 1844.

But this is not our "Frances Kidder" because the 1841 Census for Brenchley records both Samuel and Frances Frith as 20 years of age and therefore born in 1821.

Frances Turner (senior), the New Romney Censuses confirm, was born in 1826.

However, in the Brenchley parish records of 1842 a 16-year-old Frances Drury gives birth to a daughter Frances on the 4th of November 1842 and the father is named as John Vousden, who appears to be aged 18 and is described as a "peasant". Then, in 1843, 26-year-old labourer John Turner weds this Frances Drury, aged 17 years. In the 1841 Census for Brenchley, Frances Drury is recorded as the 14-year-old daughter of Silas, aged 40, and Bethethiah, aged 36. Silas Drury, a labourer, was born in Ticehurst in 1801 and Bethethiah's maiden name was Quinnell. The Drury family resided in Gedges Hill, Matfield and this is probably where Frances (Kidder) was born. It seems that Frances Drury's relationship with young John Vousden is over by the time she gives birth to daughter Frances and she has already taken up with John Turner who marries her a few months later in April of 1843.

Frances Drury was the mother of Frances (Kidder) and John Vousden was her father; in 1843 John Turner became her adoptive father and this may be why it has been assumed that she was born in 1843.

Frances Kidder was therefore born illegitimate and in one of several chilling coincidences that occur throughout this tragic story, Frances Drury and John Turner were married in 1843 on the 2nd of April: the day of their daughter's execution 25 years later.

We do not know when John and Frances Turner moved from Brenchley to New Romney but as John was born in Ashford and his family were based in New Romney he may have wished to return to his locality to work. It may also have been somewhat difficult living in the same small village as the father of his wife's child. Further, we know that their first child, Emma, was born in New Romney and baptised on the 24th November 1844, so Frances would have conceived around the end of February 1844 and it is reasonable to assume that the couple had moved to the town before this time.

In the Brenchley parish records for 1851 and 1861, there are several families of "Austen".

As previously stated, a nine-year-old "Elizabeth Austen" is recorded as the daughter of William Turner, the next door neighbour of John and Frances Turner in New Romney in 1861. Although the Census record shows that Elizabeth Austen is born in Wye, the same place as her mother Ann, one wonders if there is a "Brenchley" connection?

Chapter 2

Rural Life

For most working-class girls and young men, living in small country towns in mid-nineteenth century Victorian Britain, life consisted mainly of a daily drudge of service or hard manual work, with little opportunity for respite or recreation. Although church attendances saw a significant drop in the mid-nineteenth century *(Oxford Illustrated History of Britain, Kenneth O. Morgan, 1984)*, many young people, girls in particular, were constrained by the rigours of a church-obsessed patriarchy which prohibited any form of leisure or deviation from the strict regime of Christian fellowship, especially on Sundays. In some Methodist families God's Day of Rest was almost entirely devoted to fervent prayer and Bible reading. Little wonder, therefore, that town dignitaries and churchmen in Maidstone, during the mid-nineteenth century, deemed it necessary to voice their concerns for:

".....the unforgivable amount of drunkeness and ill-behaviour exhibited by the young labouring classes.. in the town on Saturday..." (The Maidstone Telegraph, 1866)

– clearly the only day of the week when steam could be conveniently let off without the dark cloud of guilt hovering above.

For farmers and agricultural workers, who were not blessed with hardy sons, their daughters had to cope as best they could and deliver a similar return of cost-effective labour. In this respect, there was no alternative: a farming family that could not work efficiently and reliably dropped rapidly into poverty and penury in what was a cut-throat industry, with small farming communities and agricultural labouring families fighting an ever-losing battle against increasing mechanization and ruthless landowners. We have no way of knowing which of the Turner daughters were sent out to work but children from farming communities such as New Romney were expected to earn their keep or certainly contribute to the family income from around the age of 13, when they became employable. Teenage working-class girls who showed initiative – and above all, complete subservience – were often employed "in service" as housemaids or nannies for the children of the upper classes. The others took what work was offered and that usually meant menial jobs on farms or in shops. Wages for young women were desperately low, some earned as little as three pennies (a quarter of 5p) a day. With an average weekly wage of 11 shillings (55p) for men, the labour rate for adult females was usually half as much.

The so-called "Swing Riots" had started in Kent in 1830 as a reaction to the introduction of threshing machines during the winter months, which meant there was little need for manual labour during a time of hardship for most farm labouring communities. The consequences were higher rates of crime, especially poaching, as manual workers had no choice other than to steal to feed their often large families. The riots were named after the threatening "Captain Swing" letters that had been sent to farmers and landowners by desperate labour groups. The disturbances were mainly the result of the political and economic instability in the post-Napoleonic War years and of the import of Irish "Navvie" gangs for cheap labour. Throughout the 1830s and early 1840s, farm labourers in Kent had to obtain work where they could – usually by word of mouth – and this often meant traipsing the county from village to village, a possible reason for John Turner's presence in Brenchley in 1842.

For the children of working-class families in the mid-nineteenth century, education was not necessarily a priority as most schools, which were mainly funded by charitable grants or donations from wealthy benefactors, had a choice of which pupils they admitted. These were more often than not the children of "respectable" families such as local solicitors and other professionals – who chose a national school rather than a private one for their children – and tradesmen such as shopkeepers: the emerging middle-class of Victorian England. The children of working-class families were not completely excluded but as most were reared to learn about nothing but the land on which they would eventually toil, they were what our modern society would refer to as "feral": uneducated, devoid of basic courtesies and manners, ignorant of social protocol and almost completely without ambition. Regardless of whether or not an education trust or charity wished to assist the children from the poorest of families, the decision to admit the child was ultimately with the school governors and if they considered the acceptance of a child from a "troublesome" family would diminish the reputation of the school then the application was subjected to a lengthy "administration process"; most often it was politely ignored.

This situation may have applied to the teenage Frances Turner and from what we learn of her attitude and behaviour it is doubtful that any "respectable" school would have entertained or encouraged her admission; as a young adult Frances was bad enough, as a child or teenager, she may have been anarchic and impossible to control. However we are later informed, by the Under-Sheriff of Kent no less, that New Romney was possessed of a good school: "one of the best national schools in the country" *(Robert Furley in a letter to The Kentish Express, 4th April 1868)*, which implies that Frances may have been offered a place there. But if Frances had been offered an education, clearly she did not accept it because she was illiterate for all of her short life. It would be another thirty years before the luxury of "cherry-picking" of school pupils could be removed; too late for Frances and those of her ilk.

In the 1850s the average cost of a child's education at a local "national" school was around 5d (five old pennies = just over a half of half a new pence) per week's attendance. The curriculum was geared to enable a child to read a book and write an essay by the age of 10 *("Education in Victorian England", et al).* Instruction in religious matters was also included, together with an appreciation of the arts and poetry, but the overall standard of education required hardly taxed the average intelligence of a pre-adolescent child. The "ragged schools", introduced in the late 1830s and lasting until the beginning of the twentieth century, provided a free basic education for orphans and the children of very poor families. The teachers were nearly always young females, some of whom were barely educated themselves.

But John Turner's children would not have qualified for acceptance in a school such as this because they were not orphans and he was earning a reasonable wage by the standards of the 1850s. Clearly, if he chose to do so, he could have afforded a few pence a week out of a basic wage of circa 11 shillings for the education of at least two or possibly three of his children. It seems likely therefore that John and Frances Turner considered their daughters nothing more than marriage fodder and any money spent on an education that would probably not be used would be a waste of a limited income.

The Elementary Education Act of 1870 *("Forster's Education Act" – introduced by Liberal MP, William Forster),* which attempted to educate working-class children, was opposed – ironically – mainly by working-class families because they feared that if their children were encouraged to read and write, and to gain inspiration from literature, they would lose them to other vocations. It wasn't until 1880 that all children were compulsorily educated until at least the age of twelve. Even then, boys were afforded a better education than their female counterparts

Hythe parish records showing the baptism of William Henry Kidder on the 7th of November 1828.

Frances Kidder's Birth Certificate issued by the District of Brenchley. Her mother is 17-year-old Frances Drury and her father is local "peasant", 18-year-old John Vousden.

Burial Register entry (by Coroner's Warrant) for Louisa Kidder-Staples, dated 30th August 1867.

1861 Hythe Census recording William Kidder, Eliza Staples and Louisa living in Theatre Street.

Gedges Hill, Matfield – where Frances Kidder was born.

Dymchurch Road, New Romney – the home of the Turners.

Town and Port of New Romney in Kent to wit.

The **Information** and **Application** of *Frances Turner* ———————————— Single Woman, residing at *New Romney* ———————— in the County of *Kent* ———————————— before me, the undersigned, one of Her Majesty's Justices of the Peace acting for the (¹) ~~Petty Sessional Division of~~ *Said Town and Port* ~~in the said County of~~ ———————— in which she resides, this *twenty third* Day of *January* in the Year of our Lord One Thousand Eight Hundred and *sixty five* **Who saith**, that she hath been delivered of a Bastard Child since the passing of the Act of the Eighth Year of the Reign of Her present Majesty, intituled " An Act for the further Amendment of the Laws relating to the Poor in England," and within Twelve Calendar Months before this Day, *to wit*, on the *twenty sixth* Day of *December*, in the Year of our Lord One Thousand Eight Hundred and *sixty four* and alleges that one *William Kidder* ———————— of *Hythe* ———————————— in the County of *Kent* ————————, *Green Grocer* is the Father of such Child, and **maketh Application** to me for a Summons to be served upon the said *William Kidder* ———————————————— to appear at the Petty Session to be holden for the *Petty Sessional Division* (²) *Said Town and Port* in which I usually **act**, to answer such Complaint as she shall then and there make touching the Premises.

The mark + of,
Frances Turner.

Exhibited *before me the Day and Year first above written* - - -

Bastards (after birth) 3.
(8 Vict. c. 10.)
Application for a summons
by a woman after birth.

LONDON :
SHAW AND SONS,
Law Publishers,

The Summons of Affiliation issued by Frances Turner against "William Kidder of Hythe" at New Romney Magistrates Court, 23rd January 1865. Frances has 'signed' with an "x".

Where Frances stood when she issued the Summons of Affiliation and when she was remanded, charged with wilful murder.

Marriage Certificate of William Kidder and Frances Turner, St Leonard's, Hythe, 1st February 1865.

St Leonard's parish church, Hythe, where William and Frances were married.

Theatre Street, Hythe – marital home of William and Frances Kidder: "the neighbours from hell".

Blackhouse Hill, Hythe – where Frances was dragged 50 yards.

Dymchurch – where Frances unexpectedly met friends.

The site of Cobb's Bridge from the Dymchurch Road.

The site of Cobb's Bridge and the ditch where Frances drowned Louisa.

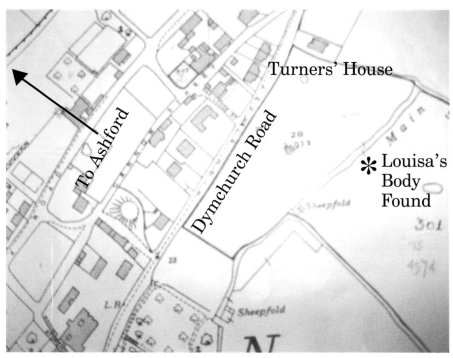

The general location of the murder.

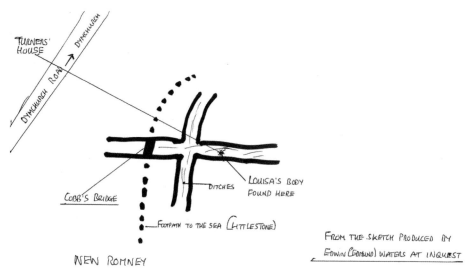

Sketch of murder scene. Provided in Edmund Waters' deposition at New Romney Magistrates Court. "X" marks the spot just past Cobb's Bridge.

The Ship Inn (now Hotel) where Louisa's body was taken.

Cannon Street, New Romney – at the rear of the Turners' house.

New Romney Town Hall and Courthouse.

New Romney lock-up.

Inside door of lock-up

New Romney Magistrates Court – unchanged since the nineteenth century.

The old Ashford police station where Frances was treated for "fits".

The old coach road through Hothfield Common – near where Eliza Staples was born and on which Frances travelled on her final journey.

Maidstone County court, now a lecture room. The view from where Frances stood, facing Judge Byles.

The actual dock rails behind which Frances stood.

The holding cell at Maidstone County Court.

Trumpet Bridge stream, where Sophia Usher dropped her baby.

The main gate of Maidstone Prison where Frances Kidder was publicly hanged.

St Mary's churchyard, Sellindge, where Louisa rests with her mother Eliza.

XXI

FOR SALE,

A COCK and TWO HENS of the White Bramah Pootra; 11 months old. — Apply at the office of this paper.

FOR SALE,

A WELL-BRED BAY MARE, with black points. Stands 15 hands, 2 inches; five years old; quiet to ride or drive; particularly suitable for a lady to drive.—Address, A.B., Post Office, Wye.

TO HOP GROWERS.

FOR SALE,

ABOUT 6,000 12ft., and 3,000 10ft. HOP POLES, lying in Lyminge Park Plantation. Can be delivered to Westenhanger Station or Canterbury.—Apply to Mr. Thomas Chaplin, Lyminge Park Farm, Elham, near Canterbury.

FOR SALE,

ABOUT 40 Sacks of ROCK and FLUKE POTATOES, at W. H. Kidder's, Hythe.

FOR SALE,

A FEW thousand 12-feet and 14-feet Hop Poles, ready sharped for sticking.—Apply to J. Clark, Kennington.

FOR SALE,

A ONE-HORSE VAN, a bargain.—Apply to John Fagg, Smeeth.

FOR SALE,

ABOUT 3,000 14ft. and 3,000 12ft. Hop Poles.—Enquire of Mr. Hayho, Tower Farm, Molash.

FOR SALE,

60 TON of Mangold Wurtzel.—Apply to Thos. Lowes, Brenzett Place Farm, near New Romney.

FOR SALE,

ONE Cochin-China Cock and two Hens. Also Eggs for setting.—Apply to J. Chapman, 68, Chart-terrace, Ashford.

FOR SALE,

A MALE Kid GOAT a year old.—Apply to G. Kingsnorth, Spot House Farm, Warehorne.

FOR SALE,

A PURE-BRED SKYE TERRIER.—Apply at the office of this paper.

FOR SALE,

ABOUT 25 Tons of mixed Dutch Clover Sanfoin and Trefoil, a portion heated brown. Also, about 15 Tons of Red Clover. Both stacks got up in capital order.—Apply at Perry Court, Wye.

A GOOD INVESTMENT.

FOR SALE,

SOME well built FREEHOLD COTTAGES with Gardens; will be sold to pay a large per centage.—Apply to R. Peters, builder, Brewer-street, Ashford.

FOR SALE,

A BROWN MARE, 16 hands high, fit for farm work or van. Also TWO COWS, ONE HEIFER, just Calved; the other three years old, in calf.—Apply to Mr. T. Buss, New Romney.

FOR SALE, A BARGAIN.

2 DOG CARTS, by first-rate builders, in good condition, at less than half their cost. One at £20, one at £10. Sold to make room.—Apply to Hicks and Son, Rye.

CHAPEL FITTINGS, AT HYTHE.

TO BE SOLD BY TENDER.

THE FITTINGS of a SMALL CHAPEL, comprising seats for about 100 persons, gallery, pulpit, and lights.—Tenders to be sent to W. S. Smith, Esq., solicitor, Hythe. The fittings to be removed by the 11th April next.

HORTON PARK.

TO BE SOLD,

ABOUT 60 ELM TREES, well-adapted for boat building, and about 12 ASH TREES.—Enquire of the bailiff, Mr. Foreman, at Horton Park.

NOTICE.

TO BE DISPOSED OF,

AT swarming, several first swarms of BEES, of a good stock.—Address, Mr. Buckland, the Beacon, Benenden, Kent.

TO BE LET,

IMMEDIATELY, a Six Roomed HOUSE, at South Ashford.—Apply at the office of this paper.

TO BE LET,

AT SOUTH ASHFORD,

A GROCERY BUSINESS, well Situate for an active man. Rent £18.—Apply to Mr. Redman, Auctioneer, Ashford.

EXECUTION AT MAIDSTONE.

The wretched woman, Frances Kidder, suffered the extreme penalty of the law on Thursday last. Our readers are well acquainted with the circumstances of the crime she committed, the victim being her step daughter. When the unhappy woman was removed from the dock the stolid demeanour which she had manifested during the trial left her and she burst into tears, once or twice screaming out so loud as to be heard in court. She, however, soon regained her usual composure, and up to the day on which her death warrant was read to her she manifested an unusual amount of quietness. She was, however, sometimes very sullen and difficult to deal with. She took her meals regularly, and listened to the ministrations of the chaplain, the Rev. Mr. Fraser, with deep interest. On Friday week the warrant for the execution arrived at the gaol, and the governor of the gaol, Major Bannister, with the chaplain, proceeded to the cell and read the document over to her. She manifested no signs of emotion whatever on this being read, but during the same day her better nature overcame her, and she occasionally wept. Mr. Fraser visited her daily, and she joined with him earnestly in prayer and other religious services. A memorial was sent to the Home Secretaay, praying for a commutation of the capital sentence, and it is understood that the learned judge who tried her, Mr. Justice Byles, was applied to upon the subject, and his reply was that he was perfectly satisfied with the verdict, and that he could not see any mitigating circumstances in the case; and the law was consequently left to take its course. On Wednesday morning workmen commenced to fit up the scaffold on the outer wall of the entrance lodge to the gaol. Throughout the entire day numbers,—sometimes reaching close upon 100—of persons chiefly idlers, hung about and watched the operations. The whole erection was not completed until about nine o'clock on Thursday morning, and at that time about 200 persons were lingering about the place. As is usual at Maidstone, the execution was fixed for noon. The culprit retired to rest on Wednesday evening after having joined in prayer with the chaplain. She obtained a few hours' sound sleep, and was ready to receive the chaplain about seven o'clock on Thursday morning. She took her breakfast as usual, and appeared quite resigned. During the entire morning she was engaged in religious exercises with the chaplain. The under-sheriff—R. Furley, Esq.—on whom devolved the truly painful duty of seeing the sentence carried out, arrived at the prison about eleven o'clock, and at a quarter to twelve Calcraft, the executioner, with the officials, proceeded to the condemned cell, and at once commenced to pinion the culprit. She submitted to the painful operation quite quietly, and walked on to the scaffold and placed herself under the drop with very slight assistance. She wore the dress she had on at the trial. Calcraft quickly placed the cap over her face and adjusted the fatal noose, the prisoner meanwhile repeating portions of the service after the chaplain. Previous to the placing of the cap, she turned round and smiled in the chaplain's face and nodded her head, as if thanking him for his attentions to her. She kept repeating the words "Jesu, my saviour," and when the prelimaries were finished and the bolt was drawn, she fell with these words on her lips. She did not die instantly, as the rope vibrated for three or four minutes, and she struggled convulsively for a minute or so. The executioner states he never saw one die so quietly as she did, and the chaplain believes she was thoroughly resigned, and had made her peace with her God. When the drop fell only the head of the culprit was visible, the front of the scaffold having been covered with a screen of black cloth. After hanging for an hour the body was cut down and removed to be buried inside the prison walls. The culprit never confessed to the deed for which she has suffered death; but she never made even a voluntary denial after she was sentenced. The crowd was not a large one [numbering about 2,000], and was of the kind usually present at executions. The greatest order prevailed throughout the entire time occupied in the execution. There were a number of strangers in the town, evidently from Hythe and New Romney; but none of the unfortunate woman's friends appeared near the gaol on Thursday. Letters were received on Thursday morning from the mother and father and from the husband of the unhappy woman, and these were read to her. The husband addressed her as "My dearest wife," and said that "if she had taken his advice this would not have occurred." He also promised to do his duty to their dear child. There was, however, a strong opinion among the officials of the gaol that if he had provided her with an attorney, and with counsel, and the long ill-treatment by him had been brought out in evidence or laid before the Home Office, the sentence would have been respited. Indeed, some of the jury have expressed themselves that if they had had before them at the trial what has been stated since, a recommendation to mercy at least would have been appended to their verdict. The parents of the unhappy woman had a very satisfactory and affecting interview with their unhappy child in the gaol on Tuesday, and on the same day Kidder also saw his wife. Some mutual explanations were given as to events subsequent to the commitment of the wife, and they parted quite reconciled to each other: the sister also had an interview with her on Wednesday. This execution is the second one at which a female has been hung since 1805, in Kent. The culprit on that occasion was one Barber, who was condemned to death at the Lent Assizes in 1805 for stabbing a man at Blackheath. On the 10th January, 1867, Ann Lawrence suffered death at the executioner's hands for the murder of her child, having been convicted at the Winter Assize. It may not be out of place to remark that this is probably among the last of executions in public, as it is expected that the Capital Punishment within Prisons Bill will pass and become law shortly.

the defendant, was a well-conducted house in general, and he had no complaint to make against it.—Fined 1s. and 9s. costs.

A Waywarden Summoned.—The waywarden of the parish of Marden was charged by Mr. Joseph Morris with neglecting to repair a certain portion of the highway in that parish.—Mr. Hinds appeared for the waywarden, but when the case was called Mr. Morris did not put in an appearance, and the Bench dismissed the summons.

Insufficient Proof.—*Caroline Smith* was charged with stealing a portion of two old dresses, the property of George Hemsley, at Marden, on the 25th of March.—The accused had lived in the service of the prosecutor as general servant, and when the skirts were lost she was questioned about the matter and it was said that she acknowledged that she had taken the articles, which were portions of two old skirts.—In reply to Capt. Oakes, prosecutor said the property stolen was not worth 5s. —The Chairman dismissed the charge on account of the evidence not being sufficient to convict.

Another Unproved Accusation.—*Edwin Kemp* and his wife, *Mary Kemp*, were charged with stealing £15, the property of J. A. Reeves, at Staplehurst, on the 20th of March. The prosecutor is the father of the female accused, and she and her husband live in the same house with her father. On the 20th of March the father went to Maidstone and returned home with £15 in his pocket, in gold. He called at several places and showed his money; but said he had it in his pocket when his daughter and son-in-law put him to bed. When he got up in the morning the money was gone. He asked his daughter about it, but she said she knew nothing of it.—The prisoners said that the prosecutor was sitting about in the public house drunk and asleep, and no doubt he lost the money before he came home.—There was no evidence that the prisoners had taken the money, and the chairman discharged them from custody.

The Result of Finding a Coat before it was Lost.—*Thomas Moore*, a tramp, was charged with stealing a jacket, value 5s., the property of John Packham, at Cranbrook, on the 1st of April. The prosecutor is a waggoner in the employ of the executors of the late Mr. George Oyler, of Cranbrook, and on the day above named he went into one of the fields to plough. He laid his overcoat by the side of the field, and when he went for it at noon to put it on he found it had been taken away. He gave information to the police, and Supt. Smith went in pursuit. He overtook the prisoner at Staplehurst, and found him wearing the coat the prosecutor had lost. When Supt. Smith charged him with stealing the coat, he said he had not stolen it, he picked it up among some bushes by the side of the road.—He pleaded not guilty, but was convicted and sentenced to two months' hard labour.

FOLKESTONE.

Corporation Meeting.—The usual special and monthly meeting of the Corporation was held on Wednesday. Present, the Mayor: Aldermen Boarer, Caister, Tite, and Tolputt; Councillors Coules, Fagg, Fitness, Jinkings, Pope, Sherwood, and Stock. The first business was to prescribe a building line in Broadmead-lane, which was done without opposition.—Only one tender was received for hiring the Town Hall cellars on a seven years' lease; it was from Messrs. Brooke, who offered £10 a year. It was resolved to offer it to them on the same terms as at present, £25 a year.—It was resolved to borrow £12,000, for eighteen years, at £5 per cent., repayable by equal annual instalments, from the Kent Fire Office.—Mr. Coules enquired as to the condition of the stone quarry, and how long it was before the present contract would expire. The Surveyor was directed to ascertain and report to the adjourned meeting.—The Town Clerk read a report from the Lighting Committee as to the lamps. They could not get the Gas Directors to remove the "governor" from their main in the Sandgate road, and as it would prevent the action of the double tap, the committee recommended that "Sugg's governor" should be tried for three years, with one meter to every twelve lamps. The report was adopted, and after some discussion as to the paving of the footways of the town, the meeting adjourned to the 15th inst.

Accident.—On Wednesday morning a man named Oliver was driving towards Canterbury, and in turning the corner from Shellon's-lane into Foord Lane, the trap upset, and he was much hurt, but fortunately no bones were broken. His wife and a Mr. Johnson who were in the trap escaped with a few bruises.

Lecture.—A capital lecture was delivered on "Abraham Lincoln," in the Town Hall, on Tuesday evening, by the Rev. W. Sampson, in aid of the fund for building a new "Working Men's Institute." We are glad to say there was a good attendance.

Our Surveyor has commenced the new sewer in the Lower Sandgate Road, with an efficient staff of men, so that a short time will suffice to see that completed. The new Foord Road is so far completed that vehicles have passed up and down it, although it is not yet open to the public.

HYTHE.

COUNTY POLICE,

Friday.—Before Thomas Denne, Esq.

Deserter.—*Angus Watt*, a private in the 73rd Foot, was brought up in custody charged with being a deserter.—Police-constable William Bevan said that he met the prisoner in the parish of Alkham on the previous day. He was going in the direction of Dover. Prisoner was dressed in the uniform of his regiment, but had no pass.—Ordered to be taken back to Shorncliffe Camp.

Wanting a Fresh Rig Out.—*John Clarke* and *Thomas Taylor*, tramps, were charged with wilfully destroying their own clothes whilst in the Elham Union, on the 26th March. The prisoners both pleaded guilty to the charge, and were sentenced to a fortnight's imprisonment in St. Augustine's, Canterbury.

The prisoners, who went into the union on the previous Wednesday night, made a complaint to the magistrate that they had been nearly starved whilst in the union on the previous day. All they had to eat was twelve ounces of bread each the whole day. Mr. Horn, the master, said that he was out on Thursday and it was the duty of the porter to see that the men received the proper allowance. He (Mr. Horn) had sent them bread and cheese that morning (Friday). The prisoners had made no complaint to him. One of the prisoners said that they thought they were being starved as the punishment for tearing up their clothes.

The magistrate thought that there had been some neglect shown by some one and requested that the guardians be made acquainted with the statement that the prisoners had made.

COUNTY PETTY SESSIONS.

Thursday.—Before the Rev. Edwin Biron, Thomas Denne,

Report of the execution – Kentish Express, *4th April 1868. Next to the report is an advertisement for "ROCK and FLUKE POTATOES", placed by William Kidder.*

THE CASE OF FRANCES KIDDER.

To the Editor of the Kentish Express.

SIR,—The public are not prepared to endorse your remarks of Saturday last, on this melancholy case. and they will not agree with you and believe that the husband was "more sinned against than sinning," because he is convicted, on his own confession, of guilt and infamy. I will not dwell on his conduct; while there is life there is hope, and I pray that he might be brought to a sense of his guilt, and amend his ways before it is too late, and while the door of repentance is open to him. My object in writing this letter is to direct public attention to the fate of the wife. The laws of God and man have been vindicated, but is there no lesson to be learnt? We have, in an important county, in this Christian country, a young woman aged 25, committed for wilful murder, who when she entered that prison [which now contains her mortal remains] could neither read nor write, was totally ignorant of her bible and of a crucified Saviour, and who ridiculed a future state of reward and punishment. She was born at New Romney, possessing one of the best national schools in the county and to which the corporation are liberal contributors. The vicar of the parish is an energetic man, who pays great attention to the education of the children of the poor. Where then does the blame rest? First of course with the parents. The father could at the last moment take a book into the condemned cell and open it, and express to the chaplain a wish that a prayer should be offered up, and could kneel down with his wife and join in it. But oh! how different might have been the fate of his child, if that book had been opened in his own cottage by himself and his wife when reason first began to dawn on that child! I fear that in this case the father had no regular master, but as a rule, do the master's sufficiently co-operate with the clergy in endeavouring to educate and cultivate gospel truths among the children of their labourers? If so, would such fearful ignorance still exist? Does not a case like this strengthen the hands of those who seek to make education compulsory, and to levy a rate for that purpose. The Frances Kidder [with a violent temper which had never been controlled] was committed on the 28th of August last, and fortunately for her there was no winter assize. By the persevering efforts of the chaplain [the Rev. W. C. S. Fraser], she was taught to read a little and had committed a prayer or two to memory. The governor [Major Bannister], the matron, and all the attendants were most kind to her, and ever ready to assist in instructing her; but until within the last two or three days there was no material change in her conduct. She was most anxious about the future welfare of her child, and it is to be hoped that some steps will be taken [if the husband will consent to it], to place her where she may be better taken care of than her mother was. I, of course, make these remarks as one of the public, and not in my official capacity. and remain,

Your obedient servant,
ROBERT FURLEY.
Ashford, April 3rd, 1868.

Dymchurch Road, Hythe – where William spent his last years, as did Emma.

Letter written by Robert Furley, Under Sheriff of Kent. Furley was on the scaffold at the execution – Kentish Express, *4th April 1868.*

18 91. Marriage solemnized at *Parish Church* in the *Parish* of *Hythe* in the County of *Kent*

No.	When Married.	Name and Surname.	Age.	Condition.	Rank or Profession.	Residence at the time of Marriage.	Father's Name and Surname.	Rank or Profession of Father.
341	August 13 1891	Benjamin Thomas Jones. Emma Kidder	25 24	Bachelor Spinster	Groom	Barracks Hythe Theatre Street Hythe	John Jones (deceased) William Henry Kidder	Ironworker Greengrocer

Married in the *above Church* according to the Rites and Ceremonies of the Established Church, by ——— or after *Banns* by me,

H. Sawyer.

This Marriage was solemnized between us, { Benjamin Thomas Jones. Emma Kidder } in the Presence of us, { William Vickerage Eugenia Vickerage }

Record of the marriage of Emma Kidder and Benjamin Jones, St Leonard's, Hythe, 13th August 1891.

Emma's grave – unmarked as her mother's was.

because girls were expected to marry and produce children at the earliest opportunity. In 1844 just over 43% of women over the age of 21 signed a "mark" (an "X") on their marriage certificates because they were unable to read, write, or sign their name. For men the figure was 35% (*Government Statistics – mid-nineteenth century Education in the British Isles*). Curiously, the literacy rate for 1815 – thirty years earlier – in England was far better at nearly 60% of all adults over the age of 21 (*National Statistics – Education*).

In the mid-nineteenth century, up until the Education Act of 1870, many children up to the age of 15, from working class families, attended Sunday School where they received religious instruction, especially regarding the importance of the Ten Commandments. However it appears that Frances was not a beneficiary of even this basic education because we learn that she was also ignorant of the tenets and principles of the Christian Church.

It is doubtful therefore that John Turner would have attempted to imposed any regime, religious or otherwise, on his eldest daughter as he may have realised that any such attempt would have met with futility. However with, at least, eleven children John and his wife seem to have slavishly responded to the Biblical entreaty set out in Genesis 1:28: "Be fruitful and multiply and replenish the earth." Of course, it may have been the case that with a fair litter of girls John wanted more sons; we know of only young John James (6 weeks old in 1861) and Charles Robert (later referred to as "Charley") who was born in March 1864.

If, in 1861, the 18 year-old Frances was not living at home – for there seems to be no other reason why she is not recorded on the Census of that year – she may have been attempting to make some kind of life for herself outside the narrow confines of an agricultural community, although what in is anyone's guess: without a basic education in reading and writing and with a seemingly independent spirit, she may have moved in circles not entirely in accordance with the wishes of her hard-working, law-abiding parents. Just over 100 years later Frances would have been a rebellious teenager, rejecting convention and authority, bored with her lot and desperately seeking the experience of another unknown, untested life outside of what may have been the social straightjacket of New Romney. Consequently we would have found her in Carnaby Street on a Saturday morning, trying on the latest mini-skirt, and at drug-fuelled parties at night, dancing into the early hours to the mesmeric throbbing of the cultural icons of the Swinging 60s. In the modern twenty-first century weekend leisure culture Frances would probably have been a female "binge-drinker": getting wrecked on cheap booze, indulging in gratuitous violence, and vomiting over a shop window in a town centre shopping mall – all in the name of "a larf"; a modern version of her nineteenth-century contemporaries in Maidstone.

But this was mid-19th century New Romney and for Frances Turner her far and uncharted horizons may have been the prosperous fishing towns of nearby Rye and Hastings or the fast-growing Mecca of multinational trade and industry that was Folkestone Harbour.

If the preceding theory is reasonably accurate, within two years and after experiencing other lifestyles, Frances may have wished to settle down and consider a more conventional life, which involved a family of her own. Significantly, Frances was still unwed at a time when the usual age of matrimony for young working-class girls in the rural areas was 18 years; by the age of 20 or 21 they were normally the mothers of two or more children; spinsterhood usually commenced at the age of 30.

Chapter 3

'Til death us do part

From the dates of Frances' pregnancy and her marriage to William, it is likely that the couple met, or began their courtship, sometime in 1863 when Frances was aged 20 and William was 34 and separated from Eliza. It may be that, at first, she was quite smitten with William; certainly the physical attraction seems to have been mutual, and she may even have decided that he was "the one". But whether or not Frances decided to trap William to take her on what she thought was an acceptable route out of New Romney and her past life we do not know, but it is a possibility. It seems odd, according to the later records and her statements, that throughout their courtship William did not mention his other life with Eliza and his two children in Hythe. However, it is worth considering that Frances may have suspected something, or had even discovered the truth that William was recently unattached, because six months after Eliza's death (Eliza Staples was buried at St Mary's, Sellindge, on the 28th of August 1863, aged 27 years), she was pregnant by William and he was later compelled to marry her. If Frances's pregnancy was a normal span, she conceived – or "contracted an intimacy" according to the *Kentish Express* – in late March of 1864.

After she had informed him that she was expecting their child, Frances had probably nagged William about marriage. However, William's previous apparent reluctance to wed Eliza Staples now assumed a *déja vu* because he appears to have been equally reluctant to marry Frances. In late 1864 it seems that the relationship is going through something of a rough patch and by the 26th of December 1864, when Frances gives birth to their child, Emma, it may have already disintegrated because we learn that Frances intends to legally enforce William to recognise and pay for his child. A Summons of Affiliation, naming William Kidder of Hythe and dated the 23rd of January 1865, was issued by magistrates at New Romney Town Hall where, we are informed, William consented to marriage "rather than face public exposure." In this respect, a phrase involving the words "horse" and "bolted" comes to mind because most cases of this nature were reported in the local press, therefore William's "exposure" was almost guaranteed unless of course the magistrates agreed not to record or proceed with the legal action on condition that William made a decent woman of Frances. The summons (which was signed by Frances with an "X") was not actioned so it will appear that William entered matrimony with the prodding of the proverbial shotgun.

It says everything about their relationship, and a lot about Frances, that she had to threaten William with a summons, issued by the provisions of the Bastardy Act (Amended) of 1845, which would have enforced a maintenance order on him to pay her and Emma a sum from his weekly income. The recorded average (taxable) income for a self-employed tradesman in 1865 (such as William) was between 15 and 18 shillings a week, *(Schedules of Income: 1860 to 1865)* although William's income, as a greengrocer or general dealer, would have been inconsistent and mostly unpredictable.

The maximum payment allowed under the Act was five shillings per week but William may have been asked to pay half of that, especially as Frances had a family to support her. Even so, just a few shillings a week would have made a hole in William's wages so he seems to have accepted the inevitable: an impression is gained that William has a good idea of what he is in for by marrying Frances, having been with her for at least a year.

The amendment of the Bastardy Act, a law which dates to the thirteenth century, was a piece of enlightened legislation that followed the Poor Law and Amendment Act of 1844 and took the serious issues and consequences of illegitimacy out of the Poor Law authorities and turned them into a properly codified civil law matter between the parents of a child born out of wedlock. The original Act of 1235 intended to use the word "whoreson" instead of "bastard" (from the informal Latin: *bastardus,* which was a term of abuse meaning: "a vicious man"). Fortunately, the bishops won the debate.

Although the Summons of Affiliation shows Emma as born on the 26th of December 1864, confusion occurs regarding her birthplace because, according to the ensuing records, Emma is shown as being born in Hythe, thus the question is posed: did Frances give birth to Emma at William's house in Hythe and then summons him? Or was Emma born in the Turner household in New Romney? In any case, just after a week from the date of the Summons, William made Frances his wife in the 11th-century parish church of St Leonard's in Hythe on the 1st of February, 1865.

The marriage certificate gives William's age as "33", although he is 36 – an inaccuracy that will be repeated by his daughter, as we shall see – and Frances's age on the certificate is correctly stated as "22". If she had remained under the impression that she was born in November 1843, her age would have been stated as "21", so perhaps Frances has been informed by her parents that she was born in November 1842. But on the marriage certificate her "father" is shown as John Turner: whether or not she knows that John is not her natural father is a matter for conjecture. However, the service was performed by the Reverend B C Sangar and the witnesses were Frances's mother, Frances Turner, and Mr William Tournay. In 1861 a William Tournay was the parish clerk of Hastingleigh, near Wye, but he was living with his wife,

Sarah, and their children in Church Hill, Hythe at the time.

In what would be another tragic coincidence, baby Emma is registered in the Hythe Parish Records as being baptised on the 12th of March, 1865. Exactly three years later her mother would be on trial for her life in Maidstone Crown Court.

Chapter 4

The Tyrant of Theatre Street

The unexpected death of Eliza Staples in late August of 1863 – possibly the result of post-natal complications after the birth of Ellen – could be regarded as a cruel twist of fate for Frances: but for the death of Eliza she may have become just a notch on William's travelling bedpost and she might have returned to her family home with baby Emma or even given her over to care or the charity authorities. We may also infer that if Frances had to employ the threat of legal action, in order to ensure that William accepted his responsibilities, then he probably wanted an end to the relationship. But clearly Frances had other ideas and with her biological clock ticking away she was determined to exploit the situation and escape her dreary – and possibly chaotic – life once and for all. And William was her one-way ticket out of it – whether he liked it or not.

For William, Frances may have been just an amusing diversion, or "a bit on the side", in another town and when he was away from his domestic problems. Although Frances may have provided an agreeable conduit for his amusement, clearly he was looking for a swift escape from a bit of "fun" that had become seriously unfunny. Intriguingly, we are left with the question: would Frances's life – and death – have taken a different course had Eliza Staples lived? The answer to that is almost certainly yes.

After Frances had overcome the shock – feigned or otherwise – of learning about William's other life with Eliza, it was agreed that eight-year-old Louisa would live with them and baby Emma at the house in Hythe. Not long after Ellen's birth, in early January 1863, Eliza had moved out of Theatre Street and out of William's life and she and baby Ellen went to live with her family in Sellindge; the later press reports suggest William had treated Eliza with abuse. How William managed to look after Louisa on his own until February 1865, when Frances appeared on the domestic scene, is not clear.

In view of the circumstances in which William and Frances became man and wife, it is doubtful that the sweet heady atmosphere of dewey-eyed, newly-wedded domestic bliss pervaded the Kidder household. And if William thought that his problems with Eliza, over the legal and marital arrangements concerning their illegitimate children, had been troublesome they were as a passing irritation compared to the problems he began to experience with his feisty and headstrong young wife.

From the records and statements it appears that the first problem was one of money and how little William gave Frances to run the house:

> "...he wouldn't let me have a farthing. The clothes I have are the clothes I had before I had him." – Frances Kidder at New Romney Magistrates Court, 28th August 1867.

The other problem, which seems to have been initiated by Frances from the outset, was her increasing resentment of, and apparent detestation for, the young Louisa. From the contemporary reports in the press, quoting witnesses who knew her, Frances emerges as a woman with an unpredictable and violent nature and some reports suggest she was mentally unstable. Whether or not her character defects were congenital, or caused by her environment and upbringing, or the milieu in which she socialised, we do not know but there is no excuse, sociologically or otherwise, for the incessant physical and mental abuse of a defenceless child, which appears to have commenced soon after William and Frances began to live as man and wife.

Although the 8-year-old Frances is recorded in the 1851 Census as "a scholar" we know that she could neither read nor write. We also know that although New Romney reportedly had a reputable school at the time it is unlikely that Frances attended it, for whatever reason. The mid-nineteenth century saw an explosion of British literary genius, as advancements in printing techniques helped to greatly expand the market for books and the written word. The young Frances Turner was a contemporary of poet Alfred Tennyson and authors Charles Dickens and Anthony Trollope. But Frances, intellectually and educationally impoverished as she was, could not have been enthused or inspired by these hugely popular literary masters. Without education, direction, or aspiration during what must have been a feckless youth Frances Kidder, now a married woman

From 1853 to 1856, when Frances was entering her teenage years, Britain was at war with Russia in the Crimea. Tennyson's popular poem eulogising one of the greatest blunders in British military history, *The Charge of the Light Brigade*, was published in December 1854 and soon became required reading for most schoolchildren. Charles Dickens' *David Copperfield* was published in 1850 and his *Great Expectations* was widely read after its publication in 1861 when Frances was eighteen. The gentle satire of post office inspector Anthony Trollope in his *The Three Clerks* (1857), which poked fun at a mysteriously intangible civil service, together with his best works chronicling upper middle-class life in the imaginary county of Barsetshire, appealed to a different readership.

and a mother, had suddenly acquired responsibilities for which she was clearly not emotionally or psychologically equipped to deal with.

Frequently seized with a raging temper and spitefulness, compounded by the heavy task of looking after her young child Emma, Frances would inflict dreadful punishment on her step-daughter, mostly without cause or reason.

The "sprightly and friendly" Louisa, that friends and neighbours in Hythe had known, had turned into a sullen, introspective child with little or no interest in life. Local people had also noticed that she had begun to lose weight, probably the result of Frances not feeding her properly or wilfully depriving her of regular meals. On the 15th of February 1866, Frances was fined £1 by Hythe magistrates for assaulting Louisa after the next door neighbour, William Henniker, had reported William and Frances to the Hythe police.

From the local newspaper reports we learn that William and Frances came to the attention of the authorities on frequent occasions and it is abundantly clear that they were "the neighbours from hell" in and around their terraced cottage in Hythe, where Frances had caused all manner of problems for William, her neighbours, and not least for herself. The couple, especially Frances, had appeared before the Hythe court on so many occasions that the *Kentish Express* made reference to "the Kidders again" in the frequent reports about their behaviour in the Hythe news section of the newspaper. In another context perhaps they would have been recognised as local "characters" who were always in trouble with the police, but from the atmosphere and language of the local press reports it is apparent that "the Kidders" were regarded as nothing less than a thoroughly dreadful couple and a damned nuisance.

In a leader in *The Kentish Express and Ashford News* of March the 14th 1868, two days after Frances's trial, she is referred to thus: "*...the wretched woman Frances Kidder......*" (whose) "*......brutal hand and filthy tongue had changed a merry, lively* *child, which could never have done her the slightest injury, into a sad, spiritless, timorous being, shrinking from everyone."* In another comment in the *Express* of the 28th of March, 1868, we find reference made to: *".....the many cases brought before the magistrates"* (at Hythe). The newspaper continues with its excoriating diatribe, describing Frances as being possessed of "an ungovernable fury" whenever neighbours or William attempted to "restrain her barbarity towards her unfortunate victim(s)."

On at least two occasions William and Frances were brought before the Hythe magistrates for "fighting" and having furious arguments inside and outside their Hythe home, much to the distress of their neighbours. (Until 1879 a man could legally beat his wife.)

Frances Kidder was not selective of her "victims", nor did they fall into any particular category; her abuse was delivered upon young and old alike, and especially those who reacted to her abuse by reporting her to the authorities. On August 31st 1865 she was convicted and fined 15 shillings for assaulting an elderly woman, Elizabeth Baker. Ms Baker, it was reported, incurred the wrath of Frances by "acting kindly towards Louisa by giving her some victuals." On the 7th of December 1865 Frances was fined again for "wilfully breaking two panes of glass" in the house of a neighbour named Potter, the partner of William's sister, Bertha. Apparently, Frances had often "amused" herself by throwing brickbats over the fence at Mr Potter's young child and on this occasion a brickbat (a piece of house brick or large stone) missed and went through the window, allowing Potter to report Frances to the authorities accordingly. Not long after, in yet another act of calculated vengeance, the unfortunate Mr Potter suffered further when Frances somehow managed to pour a bucket of water down his chimney pot whilst he was relaxing by his fireside. The resulting asphyxiating smoke, billowing into his living room, forced a spluttering Potter to flee from his home on a bitterly cold winter's day, causing considerable inconvenience to himself and his family.

Later, when someone offended her, she had cut the harness of William's horse and then blamed it on that person, who was subsequently punished for it by the magistrates: a man's horse and the equipment were considered vital property by the laws of the mid-nineteenth century.

In retaliation for neighbour William Henniker's reporting her, for constantly beating Louisa, to the authorities and the Hythe Magistrates in February of 1866, Frances had daubed blue paint on a pinafore and a window curtain in his own back yard on the morning of Wednesday, the 23rd of May. For this Frances was fined six shillings, including costs. A month later, on June the 21st, she was once again before the magistrates for damaging Mr Henniker's trousers. A witness, Martha Hyham, testified that she saw Frances: "....wheeling a waggon to and fro under them until they were torn..." This act of spitefulness cost Frances (or William) 6d plus 4 shillings damages and 11 shillings costs; at least a week's wages for William. And in a local news report in the *Kentish Express* of the 21st of July 1866 we find her having issued a summons on the 19th of July against Mrs Henniker whom she accuses of damaging her washing, clothes line and wash tubs. The newspaper, whose headline of the case is sardonically entitled "Affectionate Neighbours", reports: *"The parties have frequently quarrelled with each other and are also frequenters of the police court."* On this occasion Frances did not appear in court to substantiate her accusations and Mrs Henniker's counsel, a Mr J Minter, asked the court for his expenses, which Hythe Petty Sessions granted, together with costs totalling £1 and 2 shillings (£1.10). The court, in dismissing Frances Kidder's case, ordered a 'distress' levy on her for the costs on pain of seven days' imprisonment. As there is no record of Mr or Mrs Kidder being sent to prison for default, we must assume the costs were paid; how William found yet more money to pay the court is a mystery. However, within two years, a similar sum would not be found for Frances when her life was at stake.

By June of 1867 it seems that the Hennikers had moved to the nearby Dymchurch Road in Hythe because Mr Henniker appears in the local press himself for assaulting – on the 24th of June – a Mr Henry Middleton whom he accuses of "ill-using" his (Henniker's) wife. Whether or not this accusation by Henniker involves some kind of physical abuse, ill-treatment by Mr Middleton as an employer, or even having an extra-marital affair with her, we do not know but Mr Henniker sees fit, at 10.30 at night, to punch Mr Middleton in the face and kick him in the head as a punishment. However, we are informed, Mr Henniker was immediately repentant and took his dazed victim into his house where he apologised profusely. Henniker was fined £1 or fourteen days' imprisonment. In view of this incident and a later occurrence, Mr Henniker seems to have been possessed of a somewhat fiery nature and it is therefore a little surprising that he and William Kidder did not come to blows as a result of their disputes when they were next-door neighbours the year before.

During the fateful year of 1867 Frances made several more appearances in the local court for various offences. During one of these cases it was learnt that William had to conceal his money to prevent her from stealing it; on one occasion she managed to find William's business takings and promptly went out and bought herself "a number of expensive dresses". Throughout 1865, 1866 and early 1867 Frances's appearances in the local Hythe court – as a result of disputes with and the harassment of her neighbours, her cruelty to Louisa and her "anti-social behaviour", not least when she was assaulting William in the street – had cost William at least £15: approximately 10% every year of an average annual income of £49. With the seemingly endless problems involving Louisa and a wife who was clearly unhinged, William must have bitterly regretted not complying with the Summons of Affiliation in January of 1865, when he could have remained a single man;

at least a few shillings per week would have been a small price to pay compared to the price he was paying now. Doubtless, the old saw "He who makes his own bed must lie upon it" must have passed through William's troubled mind on more than the odd occasion.

Regardless of what must have been a difficult working relationship, Frances often helped William in his work as a greengrocer and one day, in mid-July of 1867, on Blackhouse Hill outside Hythe, she was thrown from the cart – with her hands caught in the reins or her skirts caught in the wheels – after the pony had been startled and had bolted. After being dragged 50 yards along a rough road track she sustained injuries to her face, arm and legs and she was unable to work or even walk properly for a while. A friend of the family in Hythe, Mary Burwell, had nursed Frances for just over a month during which time, Mary would later testify, she saw her throw Louisa "from one room to another". On another occasion, according to Mary, Frances had pushed Louisa against a bench table, which had left the child with a lump on her head "the size of an egg". Mary also stated that she had seen Louisa with blood on her pinafore after Frances had beaten her for a trifling offence.

It is not known if Mary was a friend of William's family or a neighbour but it is surprising that anyone would wish to help her at all, considering Frances must have incurred the displeasure of not only her neighbours but many townsfolk; perhaps it was out of concern for the children. In early August 1867, and in a reference to Frances's obvious notoriety, a local newspaper reports, somewhat sarcastically: *"Our readers in Hythe will be pleased to learn that Mrs Kidder is recovering from her recent unfortunate accident."*

From the descriptions in the record, Louisa was "cross-eyed" or had a marked "squint" and seemed to be of small build and generally slow-witted. In consideration of Eliza Staples' younger relative Celia's blindness and Louisa's apparent affliction, there may have been an ophthalmic genetic flaw in the Staples family. That Frances was a tyrannical bully is self-evident; the fact that poor Louisa was not her child, and was possessed of a congenital affliction, may have vindicated this bullying in her twisted mind.

William must have been aware of the persistent ill treatment being inflicted upon his child by his wife and of her frequently referring to Louisa as "someone else's bastard", but he appears to have been oblivious to the seriousness of the situation, or reluctant to intervene, until he is forced to do so, otherwise – unless he was completely insensitive – he would have sent Louisa away to friends or his extensive family soon after it became clear that his new wife had not "bonded" with his daughter. As mentioned: William seems to have been left looking after Louisa when Eliza left him soon after the birth of Ellen and it is possible that when he was out working he took Louisa with him. It is not known when or if William took Louisa to the Staples' home after Eliza had left in 1863, but certainly there were problems later concerning William's reluctance to pay the Staples family for Louisa's upkeep.

After yet another appearance at Hythe Magistrates Court, where Frances had been charged with neglect (of Louisa) and fined accordingly, the arguments between her and William increased and were often complemented with physical violence. As a consequence Louisa was finally sent to live with Eliza's parents in Sellindge. Richard Staples had often travelled to see William at Hythe and he was obviously aware of the treatment suffered by Louisa. However, for whatever reason, William often failed to honour his agreement to pay Richard for Louisa's upkeep and she was reluctantly returned to her misery at the house in Hythe. The cost of Louisa's care could not have been prohibitive (we later learn it was 1s 6d (7.5p) a week) and in view of William's attitude after Frances's pregnancy, where he was compelled to marry her rather than pay maintenance, this says a great deal about William Kidder. Perhaps also he expected Eliza's family to look after Louisa free of charge? Richard Staples did not earn a comfortable salary as a railway labourer; possibly no more than John Turner's wage of circa 11 shillings a week, and with his own large family to feed and clothe his attitude towards William was understandable. It is doubtful if he was fully aware of the sustained cruelty being suffered by Louisa otherwise any normal human being would not have returned a small child to such an environment. What he and his family must have felt after learning of the events of the 25th of August 1867 can only be imagined.

Inevitably it was not long before Louisa's presence exasperated Frances and the serious physical abuse resumed. Reportedly, Frances made Louisa sleep on potato sacks when William was away and on occasions she even removed these so that the poor child had to sleep on the bare, cold floor. The terraced cottage in Theatre Street, Hythe had two bedrooms and it seems that Frances had put baby Emma in the smaller bedroom and had not allowed Louisa to sleep there.

One evening, after yet another argument involving physical violence, William had thrown Frances – bodily – out of the house. Whether or not her accident with William's pony and cart caused Frances brain damage – or psychological problems in addition to those she appears to already have – was postulated but never affirmed but it is likely that it had some effect because, as her recovery from the accident progressed, her behaviour seemed to worsen and the ill treatment of Louisa increased.

The 1861 Hythe records show other members of the Kidder family living in the town.

In William Kidder's immediate neighbourhood, there is the unfortunate 26 year-old Marden-born shoemaker, Robert Potter – down whose chimney Frances would pour a bucket of water – living with a 30 year-old "housekeeper" Bertha Kidder, William's sister. In the same household there is nine-year-old Alice Mary

Kidder, Bertha's daughter. Young Alice may have been suffering from a serious illness because she died in June of this year. There is also Bertha Potter-Kidder, a child under one year old and the daughter of Robert and Bertha, and the child that Frances threw brickbats at for "amusement" in 1866, when young Bertha was a six-year-old. And finally, next door, is William's mother, 62-year-old Mary Kidder, described as a "widow". It is not known when William's father George died. (Mary Kidder died the following year, aged 64, and was buried on the 19th of November 1862.) These people would have known the "sprightly and friendly" Louisa when Sarah was alive and surely they must have been aware of the treatment she was suffering from Frances, so it is a mystery why they did not intervene and take Louisa away. Perhaps they were assured, time and again, by William that he would deal with it? We can only speculate because there is nothing in the record or reports that makes mention of them in this regard.

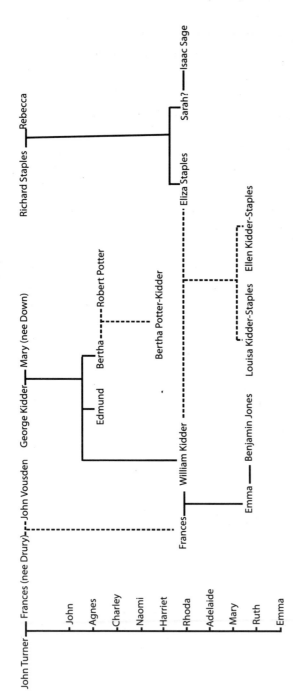

Family Tree of Related Persons

Solid lines indicate marriage and the children of the marriage. Broken lines indicate non-married relations and the children of these.

Chapter 5

"Oh mother, I'm so wet, I'm wet through"
The road to New Romney and the gallows

During the evening of Saturday, the 17th of August 1867, Frances had taken Louisa and baby Emma to visit her parents' home in New Romney, where she stayed the following week until the fateful evening of the 25th. William, heavily involved in his business, may have suggested to Frances that she stay with her family that week for a break and to assist in her recovery from her accident the previous month. The arrangement appears to have been that he would collect his family from his in-laws the following Sunday to return to Hythe. However, later reports suggest that Frances had turned up unexpectedly at her parents' home late at night and that William had not known of the visit; but it seems odd that it took him a week to discover where his wife was. Reports in the press also suggest that the Turners had encouraged Frances to leave young Louisa with them, implying that they were also aware of the suffering Frances was inflicting on her step-daughter. Considering Frances's recent injuries in the accident, especially to her legs, a nine mile walk, with two young children late at night, does seem an extraordinary decision. In her later statements, she says that she arrived at her parents' house in New Romney at around 11pm. Therefore she would have left Hythe at approximately 8pm, or earlier, that evening carrying young Emma and with little Louisa toddling along behind, not knowing that she had just over a week left of her short life. And the neighbours she had terrorised were not to know that they could now rest easy because Frances Kidder, the tyrant of Theatre Street, would not be returning.

How Frances spent her time at New Romney we are not informed but she engaged several neighbours in conversation, one of whom was a Mrs Eliza Evans who would later testify that Frances had told her of her profound dislike of Louisa and that she "wanted rid of her" before returning to Hythe. If this was true, it says more about Frances's mental and emotional condition than anything else, because if she actually intended to do away with Louisa then an admission of this nature to someone outside her family was not only ill-timed and profoundly stupid, it was also extremely dangerous in Victorian England. Further, Jane Smith, the 15-year-old daughter of another neighbour, reported that one day during that week, on the Wednesday, she had seen "marks" on Louisa's neck. Apparently, Louisa had told this girl that her step-mother had placed her hands around her throat in yet another act of physical cruelty. And little Louisa would tell a neighbour's young daughter that she liked staying with her grandparents because she was "fed properly and had a bed to sleep in."

On the last evening of Frances's visit, on Sunday the 25th of August, her parents went out for an evening walk at about 7.15pm. They had asked Frances if she would like to join them but she had replied that, as she was not feeling well, she would prefer to stay at home with Louisa and baby Emma and two younger family members, 12-year-old Rhoda and three-year-old Charley. Not long after her parents had left for their evening walk, Frances asked Rhoda to take Charley and baby Emma out for some fresh air. When Rhoda asked if Louisa wanted to go with them Frances had replied: "No, she's staying here".

Louisa was now alone with Frances who suggested a visit to a nearby fair in New Romney. Frances told Louisa to change into old clothes, an old dark dress; presumably she had told Louisa it was because of the mud in the fairgound. Frances was clothed in a smart, spotted off-white muslin dress, a dark shawl and a bonnet. The two then set out for the fair, an annual livestock and public event, held every year in the town, usually in mid to late August.

In 1867, "Mr Cobb's Bridge" straddled a stream, which fed off dykes from Romney Marsh. At this time the whole field – now situated in The Marsh Academy (once Southlands School) – was littered with ditches or dykes, all of which have long since been filled. But here, in the evening of Sunday the 25th of August 1867, Frances Kidder grabbed her step-daughter and held her head under just twelve inches of water until she was dead.

Completely oblivious to the endless nightmare that was about to engulf them, John Turner and his wife returned to the house from their walk at about 8pm to discover Frances and Louisa were not at home. John went outside the house and listened for any sign of them in the vicinity. Then, with a palpable anxiety creeping over him, he immediately went out to look for them, but after two attempts he returned without success. Soon after, at about 9.30pm, William arrived to take Frances and the children back to Hythe. Fearing the worst, John and William went to search for Frances and Louisa in and around New Romney. From their testimonies at the later Inquest and Inquiry (committal proceedings), it appeared that both men had immediately suspected that Frances had harmed Louisa.

Frances finally returned to her parents' house at just before 10 o'clock but without Louisa. Her mother heard her come in at the back door and Frances reportedly said: "Oh mother, I am so wet, I am wet through." When her mother asked where Louisa was, Frances had provided the story of two horses frightening her and making her fall into the ditch. Her mother went to the back door and shouted Louisa's name. It was at this point that Frances said, in a low voice: "She's out there", and immediately ran upstairs to her parents' room. It was then that William and John Turner returned and both went upstairs to confront Frances who was sitting on a clothes or storage box. Neither William nor Frances's parents could obtain an explanation from her regarding Louisa's whereabouts. William, seeing Frances in the wet clothes, was now certain that his wife had caused his daughter serious harm, or worse, and shouted at her: "I can see what you've been at", to which Frances replied: "I don't want to see you."

Astonishingly, and knowing what the dreadful consequences could be, William and John Turner decided to report the matter to the police. To the twenty-first century mind this would have been an act of wickedness or utter stupidity. But both her father and her husband decided, without hesitation, to commend and assist with Frances's arrest for murder knowing, as they would, what would follow.

When William and John returned with local police officer, Constable Benjamin Aspinall, an exhausted and irritable Frances repeated her story that Louisa had fallen into a ditch after being frightened by galloping horses. Aspinall then asked: "What would you have me do with your wife, Kidder?" Without hesitation William handed Frances over to the custody of the policeman on a charge of wilful murder, even though Louisa's body had yet to be discovered. Aspinall then took as evidence the wet clothes that Frances had put under the bed and informed

Why did her father and husband turn Frances in so promptly?

Perhaps because they knew the consequences of not doing so. Under the then criminal law of England, John Turner, his wife and William would all have been seriously culpable by withholding information about what turned out to be a capital offence or perverting the course of justice in connection with such an offence. Further, John may have put his employment prospects before the concerns of his daughter. Had he withheld information from the police in connection with such a terrible crime, he would not only have been arrested but he would almost certainly have been instantly dismissed by an outraged employer, who would want nothing to do with the father of a child killer, and the Turner family would have suffered accordingly. At this time John had at least six children at home and his wife was pregnant with another child, which would be yet another daughter: Agnes, born in late November (baptised 1st December 1867).

The year 1867 saw British industry flourishing as a result of "The Second Industrial Revolution" on the back of new and improved mechanization and industrial technology. But this was at the expense of the labouring classes, many of whom found themselves, quite literally, thrown out onto the streets by an employer who had no further need of them; the house often went with the job.

The working class had attempted to fight back – after the "Swing Riots" previously referred to – with the founding of The Working Men's Association in 1836 by Cornishman William Lovett who, with his associates, set out six basic principles in the form of a charter. Thus the movement became known as the "Chartists" and although it enjoyed considerable early success, by 1848 it had disintegrated into a farrago of rebels and pressure groups, some of whom embraced social revolution and institutional disruption. The more radical protagonists suffered the consequences when they were transported to penal servitude in Australia and a few were publicly hanged in the towns which had witnessed their activities. But the Chartists had sown a seed of revolutionary thought and ultimate change and in 1868 The Labour Representation League became the first workers' movement that attempted to gain a voice for the working classes in parliament. In 1871 a Trade Union Act was passed which gave the workers greater powers, including official status within parliament and the commons. The legacy of the earlier strife and struggle was that, in 1918, five of the original six points drawn up in Lovett's charter were adopted by an increasingly powerful trades union movement.

But in August of 1867 John Turner, a self-employed labourer with no representation or bargaining power other than his manual skill, and with a large family to feed, chose to adhere strictly to the law by handing over his daughter to the police.

her that she was now in his custody. While William and John had gone to fetch Constable Aspinall, Frances had changed into a long dark linen dress and boots. These clothes would be the last she would wear.

She was then led away by Constable Aspinall and they travelled in William's cart to the New Romney lock-up next to the Town Hall, where Frances reportedly cursed and swore at William and physically assaulted him. When they arrived at the lock-up, Frances told Aspinall that they would find Louisa "at Mr Cobb's bridge". Then William, John Turner and Aspinall went to search for what they probably knew would be Louisa's corpse.

Within a short time the search party, which had collected several local people, discovered Louisa's body, on her back and with her knees slightly raised, in the stream just past Cobb's Bridge. The body, by now stiffening with *rigor mortis*, was then taken on a wattle hurdle to *The Ship Inn* where, just after midnight, a local surgeon, Dr W H Wood, carried out an examination and confirmed that death had been caused by drowning, although he could not see any signs of a struggle. Dr Wood stated that Louisa had been dead for "two or three hours". In 1867 *The Ship Inn* (now 'Hotel') was also the local posting house and the landlord and postmaster was a Mr Henry Rayner.

In the absence of a straightforward admission or confession by Frances at the time of the event and her arrest, it is difficult to pinpoint the time she murdered Louisa. Dusk, or twilight, around the New Romney area in August of 1867 was probably no different to what it is now: circa 8pm. At around 9pm it is effectively night time and dark enough for activity taking place – between the banks of what was no more than a ditch – not to be seen from a reasonable distance. In 1867 the stream at Cobb's Bridge was nearly 30 yards from the footpath that led to the sea. Even if Cobb's Bridge was surrounded by trees at this time, Frances was taking a serious risk by drowning her step-daughter in an open space, near a well-used pathway, with people returning from the town fair, and only a few hundred yards from her parents' house. It is an indication of Frances's state of mind that she would have even entertained the notion that her family – and the law authorities – would believe her story about Louisa being frightened into the stream by two running horses, especially as it was later confirmed that even a small child like Louisa would have had no difficulty in extracting herself from only a foot of water. It also says everything about her desperation to get rid of her step-daughter.

Edmund Waters, a New Romney carpenter, would later say in evidence that he had seen Frances – *"a Turner woman, although*

I don't know which one" – with a little girl wearing *"a dark, shabby dress"*, at about 7.45pm, heading towards the Warren. If this is correct, then Frances and Louisa were heading away from Cobb's Bridge at that time. However, another witness, Mary Fagg, stated that at a little after 8pm she was walking past Cobb's Field towards New Romney when she had heard what sounded like "a muffled noise" of a human voice coming from the direction of Cobb's Bridge. She agreed, in cross-examination at the trial, that the noise was similar to "a child trying not to cry."

Although this evidence was damning, it seems inconceivable that even Frances would be reckless enough to drown Louisa in what was still just daylight. A more intelligent guess is that she murdered Louisa at around 9.15pm or 9.30pm, when it was completely dark and she may have remained at the scene to ensure her step-daughter was dead. Half an hour later the evidence has her arriving home in her wet clothes, as noticed by her parents and husband. This would place the murder at around 9.15pm or 9.30pm and would concur with Dr Wood's assessment, at midnight, that Louisa had been dead "two or three hours". Chillingly, Frances may have been drowning Louisa just as her husband and father had gone out on their search for her; Frances may even have seen her husband pulling up outside the house in his little pony and trap just as she had done the foul deed. It is a reasonable assumption that she hid in the trees for the half an hour before she returned to the house.

Chapter 6

The Inquest – "I was married about two and a half years ago to a woman named Frances Turner of New Romney."

The Inquest opened at New Romney Town Hall (court house) on Monday the 26th of August 1867 before Mr William Dering Walker, Mayor of New Romney, and Coroner for the borough. The Town Clerk, Mr Henry Stringer, a local solicitor (and the mayor's son-in-law) was also in attendance. A jury had been empanelled and the foreman was a Mr Albert Paine, a local shopkeeper. Frances meanwhile was in the lock-up, or holding cell, next door having spent the first of what would be three nights there. And at the Hythe National School, the first written record of the tragedy is entered in the school log that morning: "Received news that one of the scholars was dead – murdered by her mother". Very soon the "dead scholar" and her mother would not only be in many newspapers, they would also be a significant entry in the annals of criminal history.

We are most fortunate to have National Archive records of the proceedings from the depositions made by the participants, including the deposed statement made by Frances Kidder. *The Kentish Express and Ashford News* provided a most competent and comprehensive report by a local correspondent for the newspaper who was on hand to take detailed notes of the testimonies and the depositions. In view of the fact that this report was written shortly after the tragedy, it is an accurate chronology of events and it is therefore necessary to quote the report verbatim, including a vividly descriptive end of the correspondent's prologue to the case as follows:

> *"The sad occurrence caused very great excitement in New Romney, and as the tale became known the feeling spread to Hythe and the district generally. The body was taken to the Ship Inn. It was swollen with the water but the limbs had an emaciated appearance."*

William Kidder deposed:

> *"I am a greengrocer, residing at Hythe. I am the father of the deceased, Louisa Kidder Staples, and the mother was a woman of the name Staples. The child was 11-years-old. I was married about two and a half years ago to a woman named Frances Turner of New Romney. My wife and the deceased child came down to New Romney last Saturday week to stay with my wife's father. I came down last night to take them home. I arrived at New Romney at about half past nine. I went to Turner's house and they told me that my wife and the deceased were out together. My wife came in the back door about ten o'clock and went upstairs. I heard someone go upstairs and I went up to see if it was her, and I asked her where the child was and she replied: "I don't want to see you." I noticed that her clothes were wet. I asked her where she had been, but she would not tell me. I then went for the policeman and when he arrived he went upstairs for my wife and took*

her into custody. I and John Turner, my wife's father, went to look for the child before my wife came in, but we could not find it. We went down the street and about the lanes. After my wife was taken into custody, and from something which she said, I went with Turner, the policeman, and one or two others down in the fields to the ditches and after searching for about twenty minutes we found the deceased in a ditch. We got her out of the water but she was dead. I immediately identified the deceased as my daughter. The body was taken to The Ship Inn. The child's mother died about four years ago. I have one child by my wife which is also staying at New Romney. I saw her at home when I arrived last night. I gave my wife into custody because she would not tell me where the deceased was. I wish to state that an accident occurred about seven weeks ago by my pony running away, and my wife was thrown out of the cart and dragged ten or twelve rods (a "rod" = 5.5 yards, 5.0292 metres or just over 16.5 feet) and when she came home she was in a fit for four hours. And she has been strange in her head ever since."

John Turner (who was styled "the younger") then took the stand to give his evidence of the events:

"I live at New Romney and am a labourer. Kidder's wife came down a few days ago to stay with me for a change and she brought her own child and the deceased with her. Yesterday evening I went out with my wife for a walk, about a quarter past seven o'clock, leaving my daughter, Mrs Kidder, her child (Emma), the deceased, and my daughter, Rhoda at home. We returned at about 8 o'clock and found my daughter Rhoda and Mrs Kidder's little girl alone.

I wanted Mrs Kidder to go for a walk that evening but she replied that she did not want to go. Finding on my return that Kidder's wife and child (Louisa) were not at home, I went out to look for them. I started about quarter past eight. I went up through the town and back as far as The Plough. I got back *home at half past eight but as she had not then returned I went round the back lanes and got back to my house at about nine o'clock. I remained a few minutes outside in front of my house and listened but could hear nothing, so I went up the town once more and on my return about half past nine I found Kidder had just arrived.*

He said that he had seen nothing of his wife and child and he and I then went to look for them. We went up town and then we separated and searched in different directions, but could see nothing of them. I returned home at about ten o'clock and found that Kidder had just got back and he said that his wife had just gone upstairs. Kidder and I went upstairs together and found Kidder's wife sitting on a box in the same dress she had on throughout the day. She had no hat or cloak on. I noticed that her clothes were very wet and dirty. She would not tell us where the child was and we went for the policeman. I mean by this that she made no reply when I asked where the child was. I have noticed that Kidder's wife has not been well since she has been with me. She has been low spirited and on several occasions she has not taken her meals. She did not each much for dinner and nothing for tea on Sunday, although she seemed comfortable at tea time. The policeman and I with several others went to search for the deceased and we found her in a ditch and when taken out she was dead. When we came back with the policeman I saw that Kidder's wife had changed her clothes."

(This refers to the time when he and William returned with Aspinall after they had told Frances they were going to the police – not after they had found Louisa's body.)

Frances's 12-year-old sister, **Rhoda Turner**, then gave evidence:

"*I am the daughter of the last witness John Turner and I am 12-years-old. I remember my father and mother going out for a walk last night about a quarter past seven. They left me, my sister, Mrs Kidder, her little girl, and the deceased at home. They asked Mrs Kidder to go with them but she said she would rather not. We remained at home about half an hour. Mrs Kidder told me to go for a walk with her little girl and my little brother as far as Mr Wheeler Cobb's, and we went there and back and when we got home I found the doors were open but there was no one at home. I did not hear Mrs Kidder say she was going for a walk. When I went out for a walk I asked Mrs Kidder to let Louisa, meaning the deceased, go with me but she replied: "No she was not to go." "*

Constable Benjamin Aspinall then took the stand:

"I am one of the Kent county constabulary, and am stationed at New Romney. From information I received last night from the father of the deceased, who came to me about ten o'clock, and said: "I want you to go with me to Mr Turner's and take my wife into custody, for I suspect that she has murdered my child." I then went to Turner's and found Mrs Kidder upstairs sitting on a box with dry clothes on. I then told her that I took her in custody on suspicion of murdering Kidder's child, and she said, after I had cautioned her in the usual way, "She had not done it; the child had tumbled into the ditch and she went in after her."

I found the wet clothes which I now produce, and consisting of a pair of boots, a light muslin dress, two dress petticoats, a muslin jacket, a pair of stockings, and a pair of drawers. They were under the side bed in the room where Kidder's wife was, and they were very wet, as if they had been recently in a muddy ditch. I took her into custody and on the way she said: "You will find the child just above Mr Cobb's bridge, where it fell in." I locked her up and then went to search for the body. John Evans, George Parish and others went with me. We went down to Mr Cobb's field, above the bridge, and commenced searching. It was a clear, starlight night, and we were provided with lanterns. There was a very heavy dew on the grass. Someone noticed something white in the ditch on the opposite side and I then threw my light in that direction and told some of the men to go to the other side. I followed and saw that it was the body. Deceased was lying on her back; her head was under the water, but her knees were a little out. The legs were slightly bent. We got the body out and took it to The Ship Inn. I have been to the spot this morning, very early, and I found the bonnet which I now produce, in the water, amongst the rushes, close to where the body was. There is a steep bank about half a yard deep where the body was found. I measured the distance from Mr Cobb's bridge to the spot where the body was found and it measured 91 feet (30.3 yards/27.73m). The body was two feet from the bank; the ditch is almost seven feet wide (2.3 yards/2.13m)."

The next witness, local labourer **William Rand**, seems to have been a passer-by and provides yet another illustration of the character of Frances Kidder. In the most dire situation, having been charged with the murder of her step-daughter, she displays her defiance by physically assaulting William outside the lock-up:

"I live at New Romney and am a labourer. About half past ten or eleven o'clock last night I was returning from Dymchurch and I saw Mr Kidder's trap (pony and cart) standing at Mr Turner's. Mrs Kidder was in the trap and Aspinall, the policeman, with it. I saw Mrs Kidder get out of the trap at the gaol and strike her husband. She said something but I did not hear what. I heard it said that she had made off with her child and I offered to make one to go and search for it. We went down into Mr Cobb's fields with lanterns and went down to the ditch close to Mr Cobb's bridge. The ditches there form a cross, the ditches branching in different directions. There is a private footpath leading through Mr Cobb's fields over the bridge towards the sea. The ditches are covered with green spawn or moss (floating

'weed'). *I took a rake with me. I noticed in one place that the spawn had been disturbed as if something had recently been through it. We raked it but found nothing there. At length we saw the body lying further up the ditch. The dew was very heavy that night on the fields and I could see marks of footsteps on the dew. There were a great many footsteps as if there had been a good deal of trampling about there, close to the spot where I first raked. We went round the other side of the ditch where the body was and I helped to get it out, put it on a hurdle, and carry it to The Ship Inn. I have been down and examined the spot this morning. The bank is broken away just at that spot leaving a steep place about three feet high for about two rods* (a distance of just over 10 feet or 3 metres). *I think that a child the age of the deceased would have no difficulty in getting out of the ditch. The water in the ditch is about one foot deep and there is I think about one foot of mud. The body was about two feet from the bank and the field, near to where the body was found, has no path through it, being surrounded on three sides by a ditch. The field on the other side of the ditch is similar."*

Dr W H Wood then testified:

"I am a surgeon residing and practising at New Romney. At about a quarter past twelve o' clock this morning I was called down to The Ship Inn to see a child which they said had been drowned. I went down and found the deceased lying on her back on a wattle gate at the Ship yard. She was quite straight and stiff. I used the usual means to restore animation, but she was quite dead, and I am of the opinion that she had been so some two or three hours. I have this morning examined the body and can find no marks of violence whatever, and in my opinion the child was alive when it went or was put into the water, and death resulted from drowning. I don't think any additional light as to the cause of death would be obtained by a post-mortem examination."

George Parish, labourer of New Romney, then corroborated the evidence given by William Rand but added:

> *"...when Mrs Kidder struck her husband (outside the New Romney lock-up) I heard her say: "you b(astard)".*

John Turner then added:

> *"The bonnet produced by police constable Aspinall I identify as the one worn by the deceased yesterday and the dress and jacket I identify as those worn by Kidder's wife yesterday. The other garments (Frances's petticoats and drawers) I cannot identify."*

The Inquest was then adjourned to the following morning at 9 o'clock.

The Second Day of the Inquest, Tuesday the 27th August 1867

In the lock-up or holding cell, next door to the Town Hall court in New Romney High Street, Frances was fed bread and cheese with a jug of water and some beer. It is quite likely that she was subject to verbal abuse and threats from a throng of people outside the cell, which faced the High Street. The grilled window was too high for her to shout back but in any respect she would have been restrained by a local constable or court officer charged with the responsibility of catering for her needs, which included emptying a slop bucket. It is doubtful that Frances would have been chained to the oak-panelled wall; there is no evidence that chain rings were attached in the past, but she would have been under close scrutiny. There are no log records of visitors but it seems inconceivable that her parents, and even William, did not call in after they had given evidence at the morning's Inquest. If William did visit his wife in the holding cell, one can only imagine what form the visit would have taken, considering her verbal and physical attack on him the night before, as witnessed by Mr Rand and Mr Parish.

By lunchtime of that day, rumour would have travelled swiftly that a child-killer was in custody in the New Romney lock-up and Frances would have been given little peace, especially from those who would have known her and of her reputation as she was a local girl; in view of her behaviour in Hythe, it is difficult to believe that she was a model of decency and rectitude when she lived in New Romney.

On the second day of the Inquest, at 9 am on Tuesday, the 27th of August 1867, the jury re-assembled and the Reverend Smith, vicar of St Nicholas' Parish Church, took his place next to the coroner, W D Walker. Our *Kentish Express and Ashford News* correspondent tells us the Town Hall court was filled with local people. There were probably many more outside in the High Street shouting more abuse at Frances through the lock-up window.

The first witness called was **Jane Smith**, the 15-year-old daughter of a local labourer, Benjamin Smith:

"Louisa, the deceased, came and told me on Thursday afternoon (22nd August) that her mother had been trying to strangle her the night before. I was over our wall when she said that. She told me her mother had tried to strangle her by squeezing her neck. She showed me and Rhoda Turner marks on her neck which, she said, had been caused by her mother's fingers. I saw the marks were still on her neck on Sunday (25th August). Her mother, she said, did that because she did not come in from the fair when Mrs Turner's little girl did. The words of the deceased when she first showed me the marks on her neck were: "See the marks on my neck where my mother tried to strangle me last night."

At that point, the coroner interjected:

"Did she say whether anyone was present when her mother tried to do that?"

Jane Smith: *"No sir. One of the marks was just under the right ear and the other a little lower. They were red marks. The marks were very small as if a finger nail had been stuck in them. There was the impression of the nail. Louisa said that her mother had told her she meant to make off with her before she went home; she should not take her back to Hythe but should drown her in a dyke going along. I saw the deceased on Sunday night at 8 o'clock. I know the time because I and my father had come home from the chapel and Lizzy, my sister, said: "You are late from chapel, it is 8 o'clock." Louisa was outside with Mrs Turner's little boy, Charley. They were gathering the fresh cheeses off the bushes down on the grass. I did not see Louisa any more nor did I see her mother."*

A juryman then asked Jane a question:

"Did she tell you where she was when her mother made the attempt to strangle her?"

Jane: *"She said she was upstairs in the bedroom, but she had not gone to bed."*

The coroner then asked:

"Do you know whether the child was afraid of her mother?"

Jane: *"She did not say she was."*

Dr W H Wood, the surgeon, then added:

"From what the last witness told Superintendent Dewar (Ashford Police): he requested me to re-examine the body, or rather he called my attention to three small scratches on the neck. They were very minute indeed, so that it would be impossible to say how they had been inflicted, but there were no bruises about the body whatever. One of the scratches was just below the ear, as the last witness has said; but in fact it was not a long scratch, but more like an indentation, scarcely so large as a pea."

Superintendent Dewar then commented that, as the "indentations" had been made as long ago as Wednesday, had his attention not been called to it he would not have taken any notice of it. Then Mr Stringer, the Town Clerk and the legal officer present, made a somewhat banal comment about whether or not the marks could have been made by squeezing. In any case, the jury would have been quite satisfied that Frances had attempted to strangle her stepdaughter on the Wednesday and Jane Smith's statement that Louisa had told her that Frances had intended to "make away" with her by drowning her in a dyke, before they returned to Hythe, would also have been imprinted in the minds of the jury.

The next witness was a nearby neighbour, **Mrs Eliza Evans**, to whom Frances had sworn that she would "get rid" of Louisa before she returned to Hythe:

> *"I am the wife of John Evans (a member of the search party) of New Romney. Mrs Kidder was in our house on Saturday afternoon (24th August) and we were talking about different things when I asked her if that was Kidder's child that was with her. She would not answer me at first but when I asked her again she replied: "Yes, a dirty bastard and I mean to get rid of her before I get home. I hate the sight of her." I asked her why she hated the child and she replied: "Oh, because she is always making mischief and there will never be no peace all the time she is alive. Them you want to get rid of generally live the longest." I asked her what does Kidder say and she replied: "Oh, he hates her just as much as I do and wants to get rid of her just as bad." She further said that she did not like other people's bastards. I asked her if she would be out on Sunday. She replied that she did not expect she would be out the whole day.*

> *On Sunday night, about half-past-eight, I heard a screaming just as I came out of my door. I don't know where*

the screaming came from. I live round by Mr Cowin's cottages. I heard the screaming once and then I stood and listened and heard it again. It was like the scream of a child and did not seem far off."

At this point the coroner asked:

"That was too far off to hear, the screech of a child?"

As a comment on this somewhat ambivalent remark, several jury members agreed that it was

"a very still night."

In response to additional questions from jury members, **Eliza Evans** went on:

"I know it was about half-past-eight, because it was twenty-minutes-to-nine when I got to Mr Cobb's. When I heard a child was lost I remarked to my husband that I had heard a child screech. I had seen the child at play in front of Turner's house that morning and I said to Mrs Kidder: "Was that Kidder's child that was at play with your sister this morning?" She did not want to hold any conversation about the child. I said that I asked her because the child looked so destitute."

The next witness was **Mary Fagg**, the wife of another New Romney labourer, Alfred. She also heard a child making a noise but at an earlier time:

"On Sunday evening, a little after 8 o'clock, my husband and myself, with our two children, were walking towards the town. We had been to spend the evening with my father and mother. As we were walking along at the other side of the mill, in front of Mr Hill's garden, I heard a noise out in the fields. I could not tell whether it was a laughing or a crying noise; it was a sort of muffled noise. The noise came across the fields in the direction of Mr Cobb's lodges. The gas was just being lighted in the town and it was too dark to see far across the field. It was a dusky light just at the entrance to

the town, had it been further from the town I could have seen a longer distance. I could just distinguish Mr Cobb's black and white cow in the first field. I said to my husband: "What noise is that in Mr Stringer's field?" We stopped and listened and there were a good many people walking along and they made such a noise that we could not hear anything. We walked on and I heard the same noise again and I remarked to my husband: "There it is again." We again stopped and listened and not hearing anything we went on into the town. I'm certain it was a human voice. It was the same as a child would make when it is trying not to cry. There was nothing alarming in the sound only that it was out in the fields at that time in the evening and that was why I noticed it."

From Mary Fagg's description it seems that she and her husband were passing the Turner's house at "a little after 8 o'clock." "Mr Stringer's field" was in the grounds of what is now The Marsh Academy, next to Cobb's Fields, where the bridge was. Mrs Fagg stated that she could not see very far into the field because New Romney High Street had just been gas-lighted because it was dusk and becoming darker. However, if Mrs Fagg thinks she may have heard Frances attempting to drown Louisa at "a little after 8 o'clock" the statements from the next two witnesses appear to contradict her.

The wife of a local coal dealer was next up. **Caroline Page** lived in Cannon Street, at the back of the Turner house:

"The back way of Turner's house is opposite the front of my house. At about 8 o'clock, or a little after on Sunday evening, I was sitting in my chair looking out of my front window. I had been reading and as it had grown dusk I could not see any longer. I saw a little girl about nine or ten years old (that I had seen in the afternoon in front of Turner's wall) come out of Turner's yard. The child appeared to be dressed in a bonnet, a sort of jacket, and a dark frock, and she went past Mrs Crux's towards Mr Cobb's (in the direction of the town).

Mrs Kidder came out of the yard in a few minutes and went after the child. From what I saw of her dress through the curtains she wore a light dress, a dark shawl and a black hat."

Local carpenter **Edmund Waters** followed:

"I was taking a walk on Sunday evening along the back road (at the back of New Romney, near Cannon Street) about a quarter to eight and I saw a woman and child coming towards me in the lane between Mr Smith's gardens. They were about thirty yards from me. It was getting dusk. I could see the features of the woman but I could not see those of the child, because she held her head down and had a large bonnet on. It was a dark bonnet and seemed not to belong to the child. I thought the woman was one of Turner's daughters but I did not know it was Mrs Kidder. The child was following her and I took particular notice of it because it was clothed in such a poor, destitute manner; while the woman was gaily dressed. The woman seemed somewhat confounded when she saw me and dropped her dress which she had been holding up and partly turned round. The thought struck me that it was one of the Turner's daughters going to meet her beau and that she was confused and did not know which way to go. She turned off towards Mr Harrison's house and when I got by Mr Baker's barn I looked round and saw that she had turned down Mr Harrison's field. I had never seen the child before to my knowledge and I thought at first that it did not belong to her as it was some few yards behind her. I then saw it was following her and the contrast between the dress of the two struck me very particularly."

Clearly, Frances was disturbed to have been seen by a potential "witness" to what she intended to do. From the description of Waters it will appear that Frances was at first walking towards New Romney but then turned away towards the Marsh. In any respect, the testimonies of Mrs Page and Mr Waters, both of whom had seen Frances with Louisa between 7.45 pm and 8pm, mean that the statement of Mrs Fagg may have been "embellished".

Louisa's uncle, **Corporal Isaac Sage**, on the staff of the School of Musketry at Hythe, was the last of the main witnesses called:

"I married a sister of the child's mother. I know Kidder and his present wife at Hythe, I know them intimately. I frequently saw the deceased and from the statements of the child to me she has been very badly used by the mother. I have frequently seen her with black eyes and bruises on her body, which she said had been given her by her step-mother, meaning Mrs Kidder. Mrs Kidder was summoned to the court at Hythe on one occasion for ill-treating the child. She had ill-treated the child by blows then. She was punished by the magistrates but I don't know what the punishment was. I believe it was the authorities of the town who prosecuted. The child's grandfather, who lives at Sellindge (Richard Staples), several times came down to Hythe about the ill-treatment of the child. On one occasion the child was taken away from Mrs Kidder by the police authorities at Hythe on account of her cruel treatment of it and put out to keep, the father I believe having to pay for it. The grandfather said he could not take the child himself as he was too poor to do so and that the father (William) ought to pay for it. I thought the child was up at the union (the poor house) as she was at my house on Thursday week and she said that Mrs Kidder was going to take her to the union on Monday. I heard of the child being found drowned yesterday and I was not surprised at it as I always feared that Mrs Kidder would make away with the child. I have known the deceased since infancy. She was small and rather cross-eyed. At one time she was a very lively sprightly child but lately she has been quite dull and seemed to have no life in her. For the last two years she has been

growing so, I have no doubt through the ill-usage to which she has been subjected."

Quite what Frances was doing taking Louisa to the 'union' is not known. The Poor Law Amendment Act of 1834 was supposed to help those families that were so poor that they could not feed themselves or their children and had to rely on "parish relief". The Poor Law Act meant that, in order to qualify for parish relief applicants, including young children, could not live at home on charity but had to enter what was basically a workhouse. A union was simply that: a place where you would be fed and clothed but in return you were worked hard, sometimes to death. Dickens' *Oliver Twist* provides a suitable description of these dreadful places, especially when the poor Oliver asks: "May I have more (gruel) please?" Whether or not Frances intended to embarrass William (once again) by having his child put into a workhouse because of his meanness we do not know, but from her past performances we learn that Frances was capable of anything; using Louisa as emotional leverage would have been quite natural and justifiable to her. However, it may be that she took Louisa to the union simply for a free meal that day; some union workhouses ran what we would call today a "soup kitchen" operation to people who were subjected to "temporary" hardship.

The Coroner then addressed the jury informing them that they had arrived at the conclusion of the evidence and that after Mr Stringer had re-stated the depositions of the witnesses, they would have an opportunity to ask the witnesses questions.

As if they needed reminding, the Coroner remarked on the fact that both William and John Tuner had immediately assumed that Frances had caused Louisa serious harm. Prompted by this, a juryman asked John Turner: "What did you expect to hear when you stood and listened, Turner?", to which John replied: "I expected to hear my daughter and the little girl coming along sir. I was afraid that if the little girl had strayed away she might have fallen into a ditch. Any little girl, a stranger to the place, would fall into one of the ditches down in the fields."

The Coroner then referred to the evidence of Frances's 12-year-old sister, Rhoda, who was sent out with the younger children to go as far as Mr Cobb's, the wheelwrights, approximately a quarter of a mile away; adding that when Rhoda returned Frances and Louisa had gone. The Coroner also re-stated Constable Aspinall's evidence relating what William had said to him: "I fear my wife has murdered my child."

The Coroner then recalled both **Jane Smith** and **Rhoda Turner** because it was felt that their evidence did not tally. Rhoda Turner repeated that her little brother, Charley, went with her when Mrs Kidder (Frances) told them to go as far as Mr Cobb's, the wheelers. Her little brother, she said, did not leave her all evening and she put him to bed when she got home, so that he could not be playing outside at 8 o'clock with Louisa (when Jane Smith said she saw him and Louisa). Rhoda re-stated that she did not see Jane Smith at all. However, Jane Smith repeated her earlier evidence about seeing Louisa when she, Jane, had returned from chapel. Although the evidence of Jane Smith and Rhoda Turner did seem contradictory, it was all academic because the Coroner had emphasised the salient and pertinent points of the evidence to the jury and any statements about the times when Louisa was or was not seen at 8 o'clock appeared superfluous, considering that the poor girl would be dead within two hours.

The Coroner summed up the situation by saying that, in any respect, Mr Edmund Waters was the last witness to see Louisa alive at around 7.45 pm. Waters, in answer to questions by the jury, said that he had seen them (Frances and Louisa) go as far as "Mr Prebble's gate", which was in a direction away from New Romney. Waters added that a man named Kennet and his wife noticed them go there and that he had heard Mr Kennet's wife say: "She's dressed pretty spicy but the child's dressed badly enough."

The Coroner concluded by re-stating the evidence of Mrs Eliza Evans and Corporal Isaac Sage, which showed the "animus" Frances had displayed towards Louisa. Coroner Walker then advised the jury about which verdicts they could arrive at and that if there was a verdict which required him to issue a warrant for an arrest for murder, it was quite unnecessary because someone had already been arrested and charged. After hearing what amounted to an instruction to "bring her in guilty", the jury retired accordingly.

During the jury's deliberation, Superintendent Dewar of Ashford police questioned Jane Smith on the evidence she had given. Jane told Dewar that a day or two before the murder she, Rhoda Turner, Louisa and other children went to a ditch or pool called "New Cut" to play in the water. Jane said that when the children pulled off their shoes and stockings and began to wash their feet, Louisa did not do so. Then, according to Jane, Rhoda said to Louisa: "Oh, you need not be afraid of the water now but you will have plenty of it soon; you'll be drowned before you get home." Jane added that, in conversation with her half-sister Louisa, Rhoda had referred to her as "a tiresome wretch." One can only imagine what the Ashford policeman made of these additional comments from the 15-year-old girl.

After only a quarter of an hour, the jury returned with a not entirely unexpected verdict that little Louisa had been drowned and that the evidence "pointed strongly" to Frances Kidder as the perpetrator of the deed. An officious Mr Stringer then asked: "Does that mean that you return a verdict of wilful murder against Frances Kidder?", to which the foreman, Mr Paine, replied: "It does".

Although the Inquest had been managed and administered competently by Coroner Walker, the fact that he had virtually directed the jury to arrive at a verdict that everyone – including the baying mob outside the court – had required, produced an atmosphere of something akin to a "kangaroo court"; they might just as well have taken Frances Kidder to the nearest tree and strung her up. After all, that is what the public wanted and had they been able to get hold of her that's precisely what would have happened, such was the hatred generated by this dreadful crime.

Chapter 7

"I went halfway down to the seaside"

"Examination of the prisoner before the magistrates" –
The Inquiry (committal proceedings)

After the official verdict had been recorded, Coroner W D Walker closed the proceedings and shortly after he was replaced by his brother, Mr H B Walker, who was one of the town's magistrates and ex-mayor.

Magistrate Walker then asked for the prisoner Frances Kidder to be brought before him, charged as she was with wilful murder. Apparently, there was no connecting door from the lock-up to the court so Frances had to emerge from the lock-up and turn directly left into the Town Hall, whilst screaming abuse was hurled at her by the many townspeople massed outside.

Having climbed the stairs leading to the court, Frances was placed before the magistrates bench with Constable Aspinall and his colleague, Constable Sutton, either side of her. Frances was now standing in the same place where she had asked for a Summons of Affiliation to be issued against William on the 23rd of January 1865 and she was also appearing before the same man, Mr H B Walker, who had issued and signed the summons.

The *Kentish Express* correspondent affords us a brief and

tantalising glimpse of what Frances looked like when he writes: "....she is a young woman of the middle height and does not possess a bad-looking countenance." The correspondent continues: "The prisoner appears to be greatly affected by the position in which she was placed and subsequently she had fits in the gaol after her removal from the Court."

Throughout this period there are several reports of the "fits" Frances is subjected to, especially since the accident she had in July. Her fits in the New Romney lock-up; on the journey to Maidstone and the countless incidents of "screaming and yelling" at Maidstone Prison, are possible symptoms of a serious mental condition. Conversely, this behaviour may have been diagnosed as nothing more than "attention seeking", although it is doubtful if this was the case with Frances who, from what little information we have of her, appears to have been seriously mentally disturbed. Perhaps also her head injuries from the accident may have caused more serious damage than was realised at the time.

Following a brief resume of the case and its pertinent points, Mr H B Walker remanded Frances in custody and adjourned his Court until the following morning.

After another night in the New Romney lock-up, where she reportedly had more "fits", which involved foul language and more shouting, on the morning of Wednesday the 28th of August, Frances was again led into the Court for what was going to be a brief Inquiry with a view to committal proceedings. This time Frances found herself appearing before the brothers Walker: H B and W D.

During the proceedings, the *Kentish Express* correspondent informs us, Frances became "greatly excited" and then threw another fit and the Walkers were obliged to adjourn the Court whilst Frances received treatment from "a medical gentleman": possibly Dr W H Wood, who had examined the body of Louisa.

When Frances had recovered she resumed her place in front of the bench and listened to her parents giving evidence against her.

The brief testimonies of John and Frances Turner were identical to those they had given at the Inquest; as were the testimonies of the other witnesses, including sister Rhoda.

Frances was permitted to ask the witnesses questions as no legal representation had been produced for her by William or her family.

For some reason, Frances had chosen to question Rhoda's testimony about the clothes Louisa had been wearing on her last day alive. The exchange between her and Rhoda must have been extremely difficult for both:

Frances Kidder: "Did not the child wear the dark dress she was found in all day?" To which **Rhoda Turner** replied: "I saw her wear it part of the day."

Frances: "Did you not ask me to let you take the baby (Emma) out?"

Rhoda: "No, you told me to take it out."

Frances: "Did you ask me to let Louisa go?"

Rhoda: "Yes, and you refused."

Quite what advantage Frances thought she would obtain by arguing about which dress Louisa had been wearing on the day she died is not clear but insofar as her attitude when questioning her sister Rhoda was concerned, she appears to have been making her position worse, if that was at all possible.

After being formally charged with the murder of Louisa, Frances was asked if she had anything to say. Her actual statement (Deposition) to the Court – signed with an "X" – is as follows:

"I have (had) no thoughts of doing such a thing as you say I have. I went half way down to the seaside; I turned and came back again across the fields. I got as far as Mr Cobb's bridge and got half way across it when two horses came up, running as fast as they could. The child ran along the bank and then fell in. I heard her go in and I then jumped in to try and save her but she was further along than where I went in. I screamed for help but no one came. I was some time before

I got out and when I did get out I ran home as fast as I could and told my mother what had happened. While I was going home I did not see anyone. I had no thoughts of doing such a thing. I had been laid up and I brought the child down for a change along with myself. We walked down from Hythe and it was dark nearly all the way down; it was nearly eleven o'clock before we got here.

I should not have stayed so long at Romney but I expected my husband down. He knew where I had gone but he never liked me to come down here at all. I took the child thinking it would be a change for her as well as me. I have always done my best for them all. He always said if he got half a chance he would serve me out and tell any lie against me. He once ill used me very much and locked me out of doors. I had him up for it and he has been against me ever since. His child has been with me two years; I did my best for her in getting her clothes and sending her to school. I could (not) do as I would have done because I had not the means; he would not let me have a farthing. The clothes I have I had before I had him. Gentlemen, I call it heartbreaking to any one to come up and tell the same as that girl (Jane Smith) did, for I never knew her and never spoke to her. Also, that soldier (Corporal Sage) saying he came to my house to tea, which I never saw him before. I have always kept myself respectable before I was married and I have more so since for my living. I never did anyone any harm nor wished them any. I have endeavoured to do my best by everyone and if I could help my friends I have always done so. I have only been out two nights since I have been here and then I was out with my father and mother. I have not been out since till Sunday night last, when I went out to meet them. I never cared to go out here, I wanted to get home again and I was expecting my husband down; that is why I stayed so long before I went out that evening. I have nothing more to say."

During what was an attempt to present herself as a thoroughly respectable and decent person and mother and also a possible victim herself in this case, at least three points glared out from her statement that would not have impressed the Walker brothers and may well have confirmed to her parents that they did the right thing in turning her over to the law.

In what was clearly a faint – and futile – attempt to persuade the magistrates that if she really "wanted rid" of Louisa she could easily have done it during the long walk from Hythe in darkness, Frances had emphasised the point that she had not arrived at New Romney until eleven o'clock. But the magistrates may have thought, as would her family, that this is precisely what Frances had in mind when she made the nine-mile journey at such an unusual time, and that possibly something or someone had prevented her from carrying out the dreadful deed. For a woman who had suffered serious injuries only a few weeks before, the long walk at night from Hythe to New Romney must have been arduous, to say the least, and not what would be considered as a "reasonable" thing to do, so it is quite possible that Frances did intend to "get rid" of Louisa along the way; after all, she had the desolation of endless flat grazing and marsh land on one side of the road and the English Channel on the other. In fact, it would later be revealed that she had met some friends at Dymchurch who, reportedly, had accompanied her to New Romney.

Her assertion: "I was some time before I got out" – of a ditch that, according to Constable Aspinall, a small child could easily have climbed out of – was absurd, as was her following statement that she had "run as fast as I could and told my mother what had happened". The murder scene was about 100 yards from the Turner house, or "under a quarter of a mile", as was New Romney High Street. There must have been people about so why did she think it reasonable that, after a small child had fallen into a shallow ditch, she should not get immediate help but instead run to her parents' house? And, as her parents and William had testified, regardless of entreaties by them she had not been forthcoming about where poor Louisa was lying on her back in ditchwater just yards from the house. Frances was obviously clutching at the few straws left to her but whether or not she seriously expected to be believed is a matter of conjecture.

By lunchtime of that day the name of Frances Kidder and her evil deed had begun to spread throughout most of Kent. Within a few weeks, after the case had permeated the higher ether of the national press, she would be the subject of national hatred and scorn: in mid-nineteenth century England there was no Contempt of Court Act to restrict media reporting of *sub judice* cases and the possibility of press and media prejudice was not an issue that bothered many newspapers.

Chapter 8

To Maidstone

The next day, Thursday the 29th of August, Frances was accordingly transported to Maidstone Gaol in a horse-drawn prison van (often referred to as a "Black Maria"). The route would have taken her across Romney Marsh on the Ashford Road, through Ivychurch, past the sixteenth century Bell Inn and the thirteenth century church of St George, and onto Snave and Ham Street. Approaching Ashford, the prison van would have travelled through the small hamlets of Bromley Green and Kingsnorth, and through the district of Beaver to the old market town, where Frances may have seen – through the grilled windows of the van – the railway station and the marshalling yards for the first time. Founded in 1842, and with an industrial output almost rivalling that of Swindon, the station and its works had put Ashford on the map of industrial Britain. From the town, the van would have set out on the main coach road, roughly following what is now the A20, to Maidstone. Reportedly, Frances suffered more "fits" on the journey and the prison van had to pull in at Ashford police station where she was treated by a doctor. According to the press reports this unscheduled stop "delayed the journey for several hours". As there was no Winter Assize Court sitting that year, Frances would spend Christmas and the New Year in a rough, damp and dingy Victorian prison, among some of the lowest forms of human life, until her trial, which had been set down for the Lent (Spring) Assizes in March 1868.

On her arrival at Maidstone Gaol she would have been registered as "on remand" and, thanks to the efforts of early nineteenth-century prison reformer Elizabeth Fry and her fellow Quakers, Frances would have been placed in a women's section, although being a child killer she may have been housed in a cell away from other prisoners for her own safety. The prison was equipped with a large laundry and no doubt Frances would have washed her clothes frequently if she had an aversion to lice and the many other unavoidable disadvantages of Victorian prison life. Thanks also to Elizabeth Fry, prison food had been improved over the years but with a diet that was mainly beef, occasionally pork (lamb was too expensive), bread, potatoes and porridge, the fare on offer may not have appealed to everyone; vegetarians and vegans – if there were any – had a particularly hard time because there was very little fresh fruit as an alternative. In most prisons the menu was gruel (oats) for breakfast and supper, and lunch usually alternated with four ounces of cooked meat with potatoes one day and a pint of soup – or a weak beef stew – the next; all complemented with a "doorstep" of white bread.

Prisoners were expected to work and Frances may have chosen to sort rags or pick oakum (unravelling and cleaning of rope, usually for ships), which often ruined a woman's hands, as well as her spirit. It is unlikely that Frances managed to keep her wild emotions under control and we are informed that her yelling and screaming "fits" continued unabated and she often had to be restrained and kept in a separation unit under observation.

The whole ethos of prison life was to show the public – whose taxes paid for it – that wrongdoers would not fare better than those on the outside, especially honest types who had fallen on hard times and found themselves in the "union", or workhouse (basically imprisonment for being poor), through no fault of their own. In this regard, the mid-nineteenth century penal system certainly achieved its objectives.

On the 30th of August 1867, Frances's first full day as an official remand prisoner in Maidstone Gaol, the body of 11-year-old Louisa Kidder-Staples was laid next to Eliza in the churchyard at the twelfth century Norman church of St Mary's in Sellindge. Louisa's short and tragic life was over and she was now at peace with the mother who loved her.

Prison life in the 1860s did not permit casual conversation between prisoners on pain of a flogging; the theory being that inmates could discuss which other crimes they would commit once they were released and would also pass on instructions of escape plans. This no-speaking rule would not have bothered the naturally anti-social Frances too much; in any case she would have opted for a measure of solitary confinement in view of the seriousness of her offence.

For exercise most prisons employed a "ropewalk" system whereby prisoners would walk, sometimes in a large circle, holding a knotted rope with the knots approximately 15 feet (circa 5 metres) apart.

In her confinement Frances was frequently visited by the prison chaplain, the Reverend William Fraser, who seems to have taken an interest in her. After discovering she was completely illiterate he taught her to read and write a little and gave her instruction in the Bible and religious matters, of which she also appeared to be generally ignorant. Even when Frances attended chapel, to which she became an ardent devotee, she could not converse with like-minded worshippers and had to keep her face towards the chaplain: throughout the ensuing months the story of Jesus and of God's forgiveness of sinners would be an indispensable comfort in what was now the diminishing life of Mrs Frances Kidder.

Not surprisingly, the case had attracted notoriety not only in Kent but throughout the country, and Frances had been accused of being every personification of evil from that of Satan's daughter to a practising witch. Many people in Kent, and in Hythe and New Romney in particular, were questioning why there should be a trial at all when it was clear what Frances's punishment should be. The rush to judgment had begun, but justice would have to wait a while.

Chapter 9

Why did she do it?

From the testimonies in the depositions there is no doubt that Frances Kidder was a truly awful woman. To subject a young, defenceless girl to the kind of treatment described by the witnesses is indicative of a personality that was, at the very least, wicked and completely abnormal.

To the twenty-first century criminal psychologist, Frances Kidder's behaviour would have labels; it would have been indexed in a catalogue of personality disorders, character defects, and any number of mental or psychological illnesses, many of which may or may not be considered treatable. But to the nineteenth century mind-set, and certainly according to the prevailing criminal law, Frances Kidder was an evil woman who was possessed of evil intent and the British public expected her to pay for her evil act with her miserable life.

It is quite plausible that one of the reasons – apart from what appears to have been a natural wickedness – for Frances's incomprehensible cruelty, lies in her own illegitimate birth. Did her mother and adoptive father tell Frances that she was not John's daughter before her wedding to William? If this was the case, it may explain her overt and demonstrable hatred of "bastards" – as she herself was one. An obvious indication is her frequent condemnation of Louisa as "other people's bastard" and a "dirty bastard", especially during her conversation with New Romney neighbour, Eliza Evans. William was not named as Louisa's father on her birth certificate; it is therefore by no means certain but definitely a possibility that Louisa was the product of a relationship or an accidental pregnancy by Eliza Staples with another man in Sellindge. If this was so then William found himself in exactly the same position as John Turner when he was in Brenchley and took Frances Drury as his wife and the future murderess, baby Frances, as his child. If Louisa was born a bastard and was still a bastard when William was with Eliza Staples then Frances's condemnation of her was understandable, if unacceptable; it was hardly Louisa's fault that she was born in such circumstances.

Although we have only the testimony of her sister to afford us a brief insight into her earlier life it appears that Frances was not cruel or spiteful towards her own younger family members or other children in New Romney, otherwise this would have emerged before the trial; certainly it would have been referred to by the local (hostile) press and later by prosecuting counsel. But in 1866 she had "amused" herself by throwing bricks at 6-year-old Bertha Potter-Kidder, the child of Robert Potter and William's sister: an almost identical situation to that which Frances had "discovered" when William told her about his earlier life with Eliza and their two children. As Bertha was also born out of wedlock, Frances's cruelty towards her may have been a reaction to what she perceived as the social evil of "bastardy": children that were not the product of a conventional parentage – such as herself. It is possible therefore that she transferred her own self-loathing relating to her own birth circumstances to other children found to be in what she considered a similar "socially unacceptable" situation. By marrying William and thereby giving her child Emma a "respectable" birthright – even though it entailed going to the extreme of issuing a Summons of Affiliation – Frances may have thought that this had put a distance between her and the stigma of her illegitimacy once and for all; a 'cleansing' by proxy.

Chapter 10

The Trial, 12th March 1868

Frances Kidder went on trial for her life at the Crown Court, Maidstone Assizes (now a lecture room at County Hall), on the 12th of March 1868, before a jury of twelve men and Stowmarket-born, 69 year-old Judge Sir John Barnard Byles. The judge was a respected author of several books on law and economics; his speciality was bills of exchange and one of his works was commonly referred to as "Byles on Bills". He was regarded as a judge of the "old school" and was insistent on court protocol. However, he enjoyed a reputation for judicial perception and fairness.

Judge Byles had arrived in Maidstone by train earlier in the week for the Lent (Spring) Assizes and the reception afforded him was similar to the pomp and circumstance enjoyed by a medieval Pope. After attending a church service at All Saints, Byles made lengthy comments to the local press about the cases he was to hear, all of which were published – something that would not have been allowed in our modern judicial system (because of the Contempt of Court Act 1981) – and even gave details of: "the most serious case of all, involving the woman known as Frances Kidder"; no doubt the jury members would have been interested to learn in advance the gruesome details of a case on which they were about to sit in judgment. The first case of the Lent Assizes was heard on Tuesday, the 10th of March. The case of *Regina* -v-*Kidder* was set down for the morning of Thursday, the 12th.

In the early evening of Wednesday the 11th, Frances reportedly suffered another bout of "fits" and was comforted by the Reverend Fraser. At around 10 am the following morning she was led through the gaol and brought into court and ordered to stand in the dock, facing Justice Byles, with the jury to her right.

The jury was comprised of twelve local men: James Austen, James Brice, James Brothers, George Brown, Joseph Brown, William Brown, William Bryant, James Buckland, William Bune, Henry Briggs, Henry Collins, and John Clinch. As the names were in an alphabetical order, not exceeding the letter "C", it is assumed that the men were taken from some census list or a local address roll; a panel of jurors first out of the hat from "A" to "C".

A newspaper report said that Frances had fair hair and was "well-proportioned" and "stout": gentle euphemisms for "fat". Lounging around on a rope-bed in a prison cell feasting on bread, beef, potatoes and bowls of porridge could not have helped maintain a sylph-like figure. And the *Kentish Express*, perhaps unkindly, commented on how much weight she had put on since her appearance at New Romney magistrates court the previous August when she was described as: "of middle height ....and does not possess a bad-looking countenance..." The average height of a British female in Victorian England has been stated as between 5 feet 4 inches and 5 feet 5 inches, or 166 cms; what is meant by "middle height" is not clear.

To defend her Frances had been afforded, by virtue of the Prisoners' Counsel Act 1836, and by order of Justice Byles, a local Assize judge, Sir W F Channell. He was assisted by the 28-year-old The Hon. Edward Stanhope, son of the 5th Earl of Stanhope, and a Kent cricketer. No defence team had been arranged for Frances by William or her family and Channell – appointed at short notice – had read the brief of the case only that morning. The leading prosecutor was 38-year-old Cambridge University educated Mr Robert John Biron[1], the son of the Reverend Edwin Biron, the vicar of Lympne. Robert Biron's brother, Henry Brydges Biron, was also a Kent cricketer. Mr Biron was assisted by a Mr Dering, a scion of the old and very wealthy Pluckley, Kent family. Frances was no stranger to the Birons: she had appeared twice in front of the Rev. Edwin Biron, who was chairman of Hythe Petty Sessions at the time, and on one occasion Robert Biron had been present in the Hythe Court in relation to another matter.

Biron opened the prosecution case with evidence of the frequent physical and mental abuse of Louisa, which included allegations of Frances's threats to kill and "get rid" of her step-daughter.

From the list of Depositions, it appears that William did not give evidence against his wife at the trial.

The evidence of Isaac Sage

Mr Isaac Sage confirmed that he was a corporal in the Hythe School of Musketry who was married to a sister (possibly Sarah) of Eliza Staples, the mother of Louisa. He stated that he was a relation to Louisa by marriage to her aunt and that he had known her since she was an infant. Sage's testimony was basically identical to that which he gave at the Inquest at New Romney on the 27th of August last. In addition he said that he had seen "a significant change" in Louisa and her general health since Frances had begun to live with William in Hythe.

The evidence of Mary Burwell

Mary was the neighbour who had nursed Frances for over a month after her accident when she had fallen from William's pony and trap in mid July of 1867

Mary testified that she had seen Frances "shove" Louisa from one room to another and, on one occasion, the little girl had been pushed or thrown against a bench table which had left a lump on her head "the size of an egg".

One morning, when Mary was downstairs bringing in firewood, she had heard Frances upstairs beating Louisa. Soon after, the child had run screaming downstairs towards Mary, her little apron splattered with blood from wounds to her face and head. Mary said that Frances would "sometimes give the child food and sometimes not." On another occasion, Mary had gone to collect a pail of water from the yard and when she returned she saw Louisa "covered in blood, and all the neighbours had come out." Mary said that, when she had challenged Frances about her treatment of Louisa, Frances had replied that she had a right to do what she wanted with her child. Mary Burwell concluded her damning evidence by saying that she had "repeatedly" heard Frances say she wanted to poison Louisa and "do away" with her and further, she had heard Frances say to William that if he did not take the child away she would "make off with it and him too".

In a somewhat lukewarm response, Mr Channell responded that Frances had not meant to murder the child, rather that she was "in a passion" when she had said these words.

The evidence of William Henniker

William Henniker was variously described as a "scale maker", a carpenter, and a "tool-maker". Two years before, in 1866, he had been the next-door neighbour and had been "on good terms" with William Kidder, although he had entered the house on only one occasion to read William a letter addressed to him: clearly, William was as illiterate as Frances, although he could sign his name. Henniker said he had begun to hear the regular beating of a child and had also heard Frances screaming at Louisa that if she ever told her father anything she would break her neck. Henniker told the court that Louisa had often been thrown out of the house late at night, sometimes on bitterly cold nights, when

William was not there and he had taken her in and had fed her until William had returned. Henniker concluded his evidence by telling the court that he had taken Louisa to the local police who had charged Frances with neglect. She had appeared before the Hythe magistrates, where she (and William) was fined.

Mr Channell's (unhelpful) response was that the ill treatment of Louisa generally occurred when William went to fetch his pony.

The evidence of Mary Turner

What Frances must have thought seeing her 20-year-old sister standing in the witness box can only be imagined; they seem to have been close as Mary had often visited Frances at Hythe.

After confirming that she was the sister of the prisoner, Mary testified that she had regularly visited Frances at the house in Hythe after Frances and William had married. When questioned by Mr Biron about Frances's violence towards Louisa, Mary had replied that she had seen her "slap her face" but not ill-use her in any other way, "except by expressions". Mary went on, presumably oblivious to the damage she was doing, by stating that she had heard Frances frequently threaten to drown Louisa, even when she was "not in any particular passion", and when Louisa "did not appear to be doing anything wrong".

Mary's final statements from the witness box could hardly have been more damning even if she had tried. Recalling a conversation with Frances on the morning of Saturday, the 24th of August, the day before the murder: "She (Frances) said the child should not go back (to Hythe) alive; that she meant to "drown it in the fields in front of the house". Then, in what seemed to be an attempt at a retraction, Mary went on: "She did not say she would actually drown it – she said she would push it in". When Mary had advised Frances not to talk like that and to "think of yourself", Frances had merely replied that she (Mary) was "as bad as the rest of them". Channell said in response: "She

(Frances) told this to witness (Mary) calmly, but witness thought she might do it because she was in a bad temper". If the report of Mr Channell's response is verbally accurate, as stated in the *Maidstone Telegraph*, then Prosecutors Biron and Dering were being afforded unsolicited assistance – as if they needed it – from an unlikely source.

The evidence of John Turner, father

Hearing her sister provide seriously damaging evidence against her was bad enough, but now Frances was faced – as she was at New Romney magistrates' court – with the spectre of the man she had regarded as her father for 25 years giving evidence in the witness box that was slowly but inexorably sealing her fate.

After confirming his occupational status as "a labourer", John Turner told the Court that he and his wife had gone out for a walk at a little after 7 o'clock on the evening in question and had asked his daughter if she had wanted to join them. He had left Frances in the house with Louisa, little Charley, "a child of mine, aged about three years old", his daughter Rhoda and Emma. Upon his return to his house at a little after 8 o'clock, he found Rhoda and little Emma in the living room – Charley had been put to bed – but there was no sign of Frances and Louisa. John Turner went on to describe how he had gone out to search for Frances and Louisa along New Romney High Street and elsewhere without success. After returning yet again to the house at around 9pm, he had gone out again only to return once again without success. Turner said he then saw William arrive in his pony and trap and they both went out again. Upon their return about half an hour later, Turner said that his daughter, the prisoner, was upstairs with his wife. Turner said that his daughter was sitting on a box in the bedroom and that she had changed her clothes. "She had the dress on then which she had on when she was taken to jail. That was not the same dress she had on when she went out. She then wore a light spotted muslin dress and when I saw her when I returned she had on a darker dress – not a muslin dress." Frances's father continued: "Kidder asked me to go for a policeman with him and I went along with him. When the policeman came he went upstairs with Kidder and I followed him. The policeman said to her: "Do you know anything about this child?" but she made no answer. Then the policeman said: "What am I to do with your wife, Kidder?" and Kidder replied: "I shall give her in charge for wilful murder". John Turner then described how he had accompanied William and Aspinall in escorting Frances to the lock-up at the Town Hall, and how he had gone first to *The Ship Inn* and then out to look for Louisa's body, which was found about a quarter of a mile from the house.

John Turner and his wife must have been deeply affected as they gave evidence against their daughter, but the only description of any emotions displayed are contained in the report in *The Folkestone Express* of the 14th of March 1868 thus: *"It was very painful to observe the look of anguish which the father, as he stood in the witness box, cast at his wretched daughter in the dock, and still more painful was it to see the agony of the mother which was all the greater inasmuch as her evidence was so critical as against her daughter."* John Turner's evidence, when he described how he had helped find the drowned body of little Louisa in the ditch, must also have been harrowing. Turner concluded by telling the court that Louisa's body was in a dark dress. "That was not the same dress it had on when I left to go out for a walk. It had then a dark blue striped frock on."

It was then that Constable Aspinall was asked to produce the clothes in which Louisa had been dressed before John Turner and his wife had left the house for their walk. Turner looked at the clothes and said: "The striped new dress and hat are those I left the child in when I went for a walk and the dress she was found in was that ragged (dark blue) dress." For the benefit of the jury, Constable Aspinall then produced the dark clothing Louisa had been wearing when her body had been found in the ditch. John

Turner confirmed the identity of both and the jury members – if they hadn't arrived at a verdict already – were left wondering why Frances made Louisa change into grubby old (dark) clothes to go to a town fair.

As he concluded his evidence, we can only wonder if John made eye contact with his daughter, just a few feet from him in the dock, as he stepped down from the witness box knowing, as he must have, that his testimony was sending her to the gallows.

The evidence of Frances Turner (mother)

Frances's mother now entered the witness box and, apart from a few diversions, generally reiterated the evidence given by her husband. Mother Turner said that when her daughter had arrived at the house at just before 10pm, she had said "Mother, I'm wet through." Mother Turner stated that she had called out to Louisa without reply and had then asked her daughter what had happened to her, to which Frances had replied, in a low voice, "She's out there".

Mother Turner concluded her evidence by telling the Court that: "Kidder said he could see what she had been about and said he was calling a policeman".

The evidence of Rhoda Turner (12-year-old sister)

To complete the nightmare for Frances, her little sister now appeared, as she had at New Romney, to tell the court that "Mrs Kidder" had told her to go for a walk with Charley and her little girl. (Emma would have been about two and a half years old at this time.) Rhoda said that she had asked Mrs Kidder if Louisa had wanted to come, to which Frances had replied: "No, she can stay at home". Biron, who examined Rhoda's deposition, kept the questioning to a minimum so as not to be seen as a "bully"; juries in the nineteenth century, then as now, were impressed with the gentle and considerate treatment of children in a courtroom by those they viewed as their social and intellectual superiors. The appearance of young Rhoda was essential because – together with Mr Waters – she had been one of the last people to have seen Louisa alive. Her testimony that Frances had replied: "No, she (Louisa) can stay at home", was viewed by the prosecution as the criminal "opportunity" Frances required to carry out her evil deed. The prosecutors had already established the criminal motive and intent from the preceding witnesses, so Rhoda's testimony was yet another large nail in Frances's coffin. As she stepped down from the witness stand did she have eye contact with her sister? Did she evince any emotion, surely knowing what she had done? We can only wonder.

Like a cricket match, the main batting order had been dispensed with and it was left to the tailenders to give any residue evidence that now seemed to be almost entirely irrelevant and superfluous. But the prosecutors wanted to leave not even a scintilla of doubt in the minds of the jury members. So Mr Biron pressed on and Frances was compelled to endure a procession of people, some of whom she would have known since her childhood, lining up to condemn her.

The evidence of Caroline Page

Mrs Page was the wife of a coal merchant who lived at the back of the Turner household in New Romney. Mrs Page, who would have known the Turner family well, deposed that, on the day in question, she had seen Louisa at about 5pm (according to the *Kentish Express* report; or "4pm", according to *Maidstone Telegraph*), coming out of "the back lane" and soon after she was followed by Frances. Mrs Page stated that she had seen Louisa in "the violet check dress and the black hat produced". In the other reports the dress is described as a dark blue stripe (John Turner's evidence). This is Louisa's "Sunday best" from which she changed, by order of Frances, into the dark blue "shabby" dress after the Turners went for their walk after 7pm. Mrs Page said that when she saw Louisa again, at about 8pm, coming out of the Turner's back yard, she was wearing "a dark dress and bonnet". Soon after seeing Louisa, Mrs Page said she saw "Mrs Kidder with a dark shawl, a light dress and a hat." According to *The Maidstone Telegraph*, Mrs Page told the court she saw: "the prisoner come out as soon as the girl was out of sight. The prisoner was wearing a light muslin dress and went in the same direction (as Louisa)."

If Mrs Page's recollection – some six months after the event – is correct, then Frances and Louisa had left the house that day, for some reason, at either 4pm or 5pm. This is not mentioned by the Turners, although it is possible that Frances and Louisa simply went out for some fresh air. Alternatively, Frances could have been carrying out a "rehearsal". Further, Mrs Page stated that she saw Louisa emerging from the back of the house at about the same time - 8pm - as the Turners were coming home from their walk. If this is correct, the Turners must have just missed Frances and Louisa. Rhoda Turner stated that she had left the house at about 7-45pm ("We stayed for about half an hour" – after the Turners had left at about 7-15 pm.) so Frances and Louisa may have left the house soon after. Where Frances and Louisa went for about an hour and a half is a mystery: there seems to be no evidence that they were seen at the town's annual fair.

The evidence of Edmund Waters, carpenter, New Romney

Mr Waters deposed that, on the evening in question, the 25th, at about a quarter to eight, he was "out on the back road, walking towards the Warren" (towards Dymchurch). This is the same road at the back of the Turner's house where Mrs Page lived: from the descriptions, the road is Cannon Street. Waters' deposition is quoted, verbatim, as it appears in *The Kentish Express*:

"I passed a woman and child. The woman was the prisoner. I knew her to be one of Turner's daughters. A little girl was behind her and dressed in a dark and rather shabby and dirty dress. They were coming towards me. They turned to the left when they saw me and I looked round afterwards and saw that they turned to the right. They were then going down a lane leading towards the Marsh."

Judge Byles then intervened with quotes from the deposition Waters made at the Inquest: "They seemed confused when they saw me. It was getting a little dusk. I'm quite sure it was one of the Turner daughters. I meant that I did not know which one of the Turner's daughters it was." Quite what the point of Byles's interjection was is not clear: it is quite obvious that Waters saw Frances and Louisa, who seemed to be going in awkward directions, as if to confuse any witnesses, perhaps? However, if Mr Waters is correct about the time he saw Frances and Louisa – "about a quarter to eight" – then Frances had taken Louisa out soon after Rhoda had gone for her walk with Charley and Emma: between 7.40pm and 7.45pm.

The evidence of Mary Fagg

Mary Fagg then testified. Mary's husband, Alfred, was an employee of Mr Cobb, clearly a major employer in New Romney and on whose land ("Cobb's bridge") the murder had occurred. Mary Fagg's somewhat dramatic deposition was as follows:

"I was out for a walk at a little past eight o' clock on the evening of the 26th (obviously meant to be the 25th) of August last. I heard screams when I was walking past Cobb's fields. (towards New Romney) The sounds came from Cobb's fields across from the lodges (houses). *It was a muffled noise of the human voice. I stopped and listened and everything was quiet. We passed on and I heard the noise again. The second noise came from the same direction, it was the same muffled sound of a human voice."*

According to the report in the *South Eastern Gazette*, Mary Fagg had agreed when asked by one of the prosecutors: "The voice was like the voice of a child trying not to cry".

Then, according to the *South Eastern Gazette*, the court clerk read out an extract of Mary Fagg's deposition at the Inquest: "I said before the coroner that I could not tell whether it was a laughing or a crying sound *and that it was not at all alarming*". This statement by Mary at the Inquest seems to be of a different flavour to the deposition given in the witness box at the trial.

By the time Frances Kidder appeared in Maidstone Crown Court she was probably the most hated woman in Kent, if not in England, and it is possible that, in such cases, witnesses would feel compelled to amend or embellish their evidence accordingly. Certainly, there was no question that the jury members knew exactly who she was and what she had done long before they had been sworn in.

The evidence of Eliza Evans, neighbour in New Romney

Eliza Evans was the wife of labourer, John Evans, of New Romney. Mrs Evans was the neighbour, previously referred to, who had the conversation with Frances on the Saturday before the murder. Her evidence, of course, is damning and she was possibly used by the prosecution as a "belt and braces" job just in case there may have been any doubt concerning Frances's culpability. Mrs Evans's evidence, as reported in the *Kentish Express*, is as follows: "I know the prisoner. She came to my house on Saturday afternoon, the 24th of August. She said she meant to get rid of the deceased child before she went home. She said she hated the sight of her and that there could never be any peace all the time she was living. I asked her what Kidder said about it. She replied he hated her as bad as she did and would like to get rid of her as much as she did. She said she did not like keeping other people's bastards."

The evidence of Police Constable Benjamin Aspinall

New Romney policeman, Constable Benjamin Aspinall, was then called to give evidence. It was at this point that New Romney solicitor, Mr Stringer (the Town Clerk), was asked to produce a brief sketch or map of where Louisa's body was found in relation to the Turner's house in Dymchurch Road. Aspinall told how he went to the Turner's house on the night of the 25th of August and how he saw Frances there and placed her in custody, charged with wilful murder, at the behest of her husband William. Aspinall's deposition provides a detailed account of the events from his first meeting with Frances to the discovery of Louisa's body in the ditch, together with details of measurements of the river bank and descriptions of the murder scene. In consideration of the submission of Frances's defence counsel, W F Channell, to the jury at the end of the trial, it is necessary to quote verbatim Aspinall's deposition, as reported in the *Kentish Express*, as follows:

"I went to Turner's house..........I saw the prisoner there. She was then wearing the clothes she has on now. She was in her mother's bedroom. I told her her husband had given her in custody on suspicion of murdering her child and I cautioned her in the usual way. She said she did not do it, the child tumbled into a ditch and she went in after her. The wet clothes I now produce were under a side bed in the room where the prisoner was. They were very wet. The muslin dress was wet for fourteen or fifteen inches up and the bottom was muddy. The arms of the muslin sleeves were very wet up to the elbows. On her way to the lock-up the prisoner said to me: "You'll find the child just above Mr Cobb's bridge." That is a bridge passing over a ditch. It is a plank with rails on each side where a footpath goes right away to the seaside. After I had locked her up I went with the others to look for the body. It was a clear night and we had lamps with us. There was

a heavy dew on the grass. To the right of Cobb's bridge, and about thirty yards from the pathway, we found the body. It is not still water in the ditch but it is a very sluggish stream; it depends greatly on the state of the tide. The water in which the body was lying was about fourteen inches in depth, and there were about nine inches of mud. I measured it the following morning. The deceased was lying on her back with her face upwards and her legs slightly bent and a little out of the water. We got the body out and took it to the Ship Inn. The banks on each side of the ditch are about half a yard deep. A girl the age of the deceased might easily have got out of the water. I have seen a child of about four or five years of age escape from that ditch. The body was three feet from the bank and the ditch is about seven feet wide. The body was nearest to the side of the ditch which is towards Turner's house."

The closing speeches, by Biron and Channell, did not take too long. Biron merely emphasised what a dreadful person Frances was and that it was perfectly clear – "from the evidence we have heard in this court" – that she wilfully murdered young Louisa and had made her intentions quite clear to several people, including her husband.

Mr Channell attempted to obtain a silk purse from the proverbial sow's ear and made a sterling effort on behalf of his hated client. He attempted to place some doubt in the minds of the jury by repeating that the doctor who had examined Louisa at the Ship Inn told the inquest and the inquiry that the girl had died from drowning but that he had found no marks of violence on her body. He mentioned the accident Frances had suffered several weeks before the murder, suggesting that the effects of this traumatic experience may have had something to do with the way she behaved. But the statements from the witnesses had made it clear that Frances was seriously abusing Louisa long before the unfortunate incident with William's pony and cart; many jury members may have concluded that the accident made Frances a more evil person than she already was.

Channell stoutly asserted that some of the evidence involving Louisa may have been "exaggerated and embellished", but that didn't seem to wash either. Concluding, Channell re-stated Frances's deposition and previous statement that the whole tragedy had been caused by a pair of wild horses frightening Louisa into the ditch and that Frances had tried to save her. Unfortunately, as the jury had heard that the ditch contained just twelve inches of water and, recalling Constable Aspinall's evidence that a younger child had easily extracted itself from the ditch on an earlier occasion, Frances's explanation of her attempts to "rescue" Louisa carried little, if any, substance. And in what appears to have been an act of desperation, Channell asserted that, if Frances had wanted to "get rid" of Louisa, she could have achieved it on the journey from Hythe to New Romney on the evening of the 17th of August. But this last throw of the dice was also a loser – and Channell probably knew it.

After a trial lasting four or five hours Justice Byles carefully delivered his summing-up of the case, emphasising the salient points of evidence on either side. Then he addressed the jury and pointedly reminded them that if they had any doubt at all that the accused intentionally caused the death of her step-daughter they should return a verdict of not guilty of capital murder. But the jury members were not in a giving mood, especially where the cruel death of an innocent child was concerned, and no sooner was Frances led to the holding cell than she was called back into court again. After only twelve minutes retirement the jury had returned with a unanimous verdict of "guilty as charged".

A stunned and ashen-faced Frances stood motionless in the dock as Justice Byles asked her if she had anything to say before he passed sentence upon her. The reports state that Frances lowered her head and whispered: "No". Immediately, the Clerk of the Court asked her if there was any other reason (pregnancy) why sentence should not be passed, to which Frances slowly shook her head. Then Byles placed the little square of black cloth on his bewigged head and pronounced – after stating that this was not his sentence but the sentence of the law of the land – that Frances would be taken from the court to a place of lawful execution whereat she shall be hanged by the neck until she be dead and that her body was to be placed within the precincts of the prison in which she was last confined. Justice Byles ended his dread recital with: "And may the Lord have mercy upon your soul". A doleful Clerk to the Court muttered "Amen" and Frances was taken the short distance from the court room to Maidstone Gaol and the condemned cell where she would languish until the day of her execution, which was set at noon of Thursday, the 2nd of April.

Frances Kidder had been sent to the gallows on the testimonies of her husband, her parents, and two of her sisters.

The trial and all the ghastly details had been reported in newspapers as far as Glasgow (*Glasgow Herald*, March 26th 1868), Newcastle (*Newcastle Courant*, March 20th 1868) and Liverpool (*Liverpool Mercury*, March 30th 1868). In Belfast, the day after the execution, the *Belfast News Letter* of the 3rd of April had referred to Louisa as "aged thirteen". The London based papers, *The Times* and *The Telegraph*, both of which had regularly featured the case, had managed to turn Frances into a national monster. In March of 1868 Frances Kidder was the nineteenth century equivalent of Myra Hindley.

Chapter 11

Did Frances Kidder have a Defence in Law?

O n the 30th of July 1867, when Frances was recovering from her accident, and just under a month before she murdered Louisa, a 40-year-old Ashford widow, Sophia Usher, was sentenced to death at Maidstone Assizes for drowning her newborn baby on the 4th of April in a stream at the Trumpet Bridge near Ashford town. Although Sophia was formally sentenced to death, as required by law, the jury had recommended mercy and the sentence was later commuted to life imprisonment by the Home Office on the recommendation of the trial judge, Justice Blackburn.

The jury had heard how Sophia, a hitherto respectable wife and mother of four children, had been married to a well-respected Ashford man, a painter at the local railway works, who was also the secretary of the Court of Friendly Mechanics of the Order of Foresters. But since her husband's unexpected and premature death in 1861, Sophia Usher appears to have descended into a morally unhealthy existence, which had been completely foreign to her previous good character, and which had attracted rumours of a sordid and disreputable lifestyle. Apparently these rumours, together with Sophia's insouciant attitude, had resulted in her losing her employment and almost her home. With little money, pregnant in her middle age, and deserted by the father of her unborn child, the widow Usher had hit the Victorian equivalent of Skid Row. After borrowing money for the rail fare to London, she had given birth at her relatives' home in Gloucester Terrace, Hackney Road, where doctors from Guy's and Bartholomew's Hospitals had attended her after she had become "insensible" (unconscious) and seriously ill. She had returned to Ashford with the two-week old baby and had been met by her 19-year-old daughter, Emma, at the station. Mother and daughter, together with the swathed infant, had proceeded to Sophia's home in the Beaver district of Ashford, where Sophia had stopped by the Trumpet Bridge and had simply dropped the baby into the stream. Emma had originally been charged as an associate to the child's murder but the jury had rejected this charge after hearing that she had stood at the bridge imploring her mother not to carry out the dreadful deed. No doubt the jury had also been impressed by Emma's previous statement that she had put her fingers in her ears so as not to hear the plop of the infant in the muddy water.

Sophia seems to have been suffering from depression or some other post-natal medical condition that was beginning to be recognised by the nineteenth century judiciary as an unavoidable and tragic illness that affected some women immediately after childbirth. In Sophia's case she was – to employ a modern term pertaining to such situations – "not bad or mad but sad" and it would have been unjust, and not least inhumane, to have allowed her to suffer death as prescribed by the law. Consequently, and after a submission by the trial judge to the Home Office, Sophia Usher's death sentence was commuted to life imprisonment and penal servitude by order of the court on the 31st of August 1867. According to the *Kentish Express* report of the 7th of September 1867, she had showed no emotion and had seemed to be "unaffected" by having her life spared; an attitude of indifference that may be recognisable as a symptom of severe depression. The reason for the commutation of sentence, according to the press reports, was because of Sophia's "feeble-mindedness" and poor mental state (her hair had fallen out on two occasions and she had been subjected to frequent "fainting"), which may have been caused by the traumatic consequences of her widowhood. The Assize Court had heard, because Judge Blackburn had informed them (he seems also to have appointed himself as her defence spokesman or counsel), that Sophia had been a hard-working needlewoman and a devoted wife and mother before the tragic death in 1861 of her much-loved and well-respected husband.

However, Frances Kidder was not suffering from any recognised medical condition, she was not considered to be "feeble minded", she was not a widow, her husband was not a member of the Order of Foresters, and certainly she did not command the respect of her local community; quite the opposite in fact. Moreover, Louisa was not an "infant": she was an 11-year-old girl on the verge of a full life and she had been deprived of that life by an evil stepmother for no apparent reason other than Frances Kidder's incomprehensible and completely unjustified hatred for "other people's bastards". A cynic would say that the marked contrast in the character and background of Sophia Usher and Frances Kidder ensured that the former would not climb the gallows' steps; a cynic may well be right. However, Sophia had not relentlessly abused her child by half-starving her, beating her, violently throwing her around the house and calling her someone else's bastard; nor had she poured water down a neighbour's chimney, thrown bricks at his young child, wilfully damaged another neighbour's property and made her neighbours' lives a living hell. The difference between the desolate and spiritless shell of a person that was Sophia Usher and the pure spitting evil that was Frances Kidder was painfully obvious.

From the local press reports attesting to her notoriously bad behaviour, the reports of the inquest and trial evidence, and from the statements of those who knew her, there seems little doubt that Frances Kidder was a thoroughly awful woman and any "defence" of what she had been convicted was unsustainable. Her counsel, Mr Channell, had made an attempt to explain and mitigate his client's dreadful crime by relating the serious accident and subsequent injuries sustained by Frances when she was thrown from the pony and cart a month before the murder, in mid-July, when helping William in his work. William had referred to the incident at the Inquest in New Romney on the 26th of August, the day after the murder, saying that after the accident Frances had been "strange in her head". William deposed at the Inquest that Frances had been dragged "ten or twelve rods", which means that she was bumped along what was the rough road of Blackhouse Hill in Hythe for at least 55 yards (or over 50 metres), and therefore William's statement that Frances had been somehow psychologically affected as a result of her injuries was probably not overstated. But it carried little, if any, weight with a jury that seemed intent on returning a guilty verdict. Channell had also attempted to sway the jury by asserting that Frances could not have had wilful murderous intent because she could have disposed of Louisa on the road between Hythe and New Romney when they had travelled on foot in the early evening of the Saturday before the incident.

The distance from Theatre Street off the High Street in Hythe where William and Frances lived, to the Turner's house in New Romney, is nearly nine miles. At a steady modern car speed of circa 35 mph, the time is approximately sixteen minutes; William's pony and cart would have taken no more than three quarters of an hour. By foot – at an average walking pace of three miles per hour – it would have taken nearly three hours: we are not informed why William did not take Frances and the children on his pony and trap but it is presumed it was to do with his business. *The Kentish Express* tells us that Frances had sent on her luggage by carrier and that she had set out on foot with the two children in the early evening of the 17th of August so it is quite possible that, unhindered by luggage, she intended to "do away with" Louisa on the journey. But she had unexpectedly met friends at Dymchurch and these friends accompanied Frances and the children all the way to New Romney. It is not surprising, therefore, that Channell's plea of "no wilful intent", regardless of opportunity, clearly failed.

In 1868 the only defence available for the capital crime of murder had been formulated and enacted by Parliament in 1843. This defence was known as the McNaghten (M'Naghten) Rules, named after a Scottish woodworker who, convinced that the government was out to kill him, pumped several bullets into the back of Edward Drummond, Prime Minister Sir Robert Peel's secretary, in the belief that Drummond was in fact Prime Minister Peel. Daniel McNaghten was clearly mad and this was confirmed by several doctors who examined him at the time. After a trial, where McNaghten was judged guilty but "criminally insane", he was sent to the Bethlem (Bedlam) lunatic asylum: a reduced charge (of manslaughter) was not available.

Before 1843 the actions of another madman had helped to introduce a vague – and wholly insufficient – form of defence by insanity for a capital crime. On the evening of the 15th of May 1800, at the Theatre Royal, Drury Lane, James Hadfield, an ex soldier and a veteran of the Battle of Tourcoing (1794) – where he had suffered serious head injuries caused by a sabre – fired his pistol at George III during the playing of the national anthem. Fortunately for King George (who was mad himself) Hadfield missed his target and had then gleefully informed the King that he thought he was a jolly good fellow. Although he was patently insane, Hadfield was charged with (wilful) treason, which carried an automatic death penalty. One explanation offered by Hadfield for his actions was that he had to sacrifice himself by being executed by the British government in order to herald the Second Coming of Christ. At his trial Hadfield was defended by the celebrated counsel Thomas Erskine who succeeded in convincing the court that his client, at the time of the attempted assassination, had been: "lost to all sense...incapable of forming a judgment". The legal arguments of the case, and Hadfield's subsequent acquittal of the treason charge, birthed the Criminal Lunatics Act (1800), which offered a "defence" of madness, albeit a nebulous one, and which also attempted to define the criminal law status of a lunatic, an idiot, and a deaf and dumb mute. In any respect, those who succeeded in meeting the criteria for madness, idiocy, or dumbness set out in the Act may have been found not guilty of wilfully committing a capital crime but they nonetheless ended up caged in a lunatic asylum: "...until the King's pleasure be known....", which often meant for life. The McNaghten case went further and finally there was a reasonably definitive criteria for who was mad – or "temporarily insane" – and who was not.

Up until these landmarks in English criminal law it was almost impossible to avoid the hangman's noose by reason of insanity unless the culprit was seen to be suffering from such a degree of madness that, when he was dragged barking and gurgling into court, the judge was too embarrassed to allow any trial to proceed and the accused was simply set free or thrown into one of the many new "hospitals" where he was left to die. Alternatively, such persons were transported to the Australian penal colonies where they were expected to die soon enough anyway.

Unfortunately the short but significant advancement of the English criminal justice system was not to the liking of several trial judges, one of whom was Lord Alderson. A year after the introduction of the M'Naghten Rules, Alderson locked a jury in a small room without food and water until they rejected the defence of M'Naghten and returned with a verdict of guilty of wilful murder by an accused wife killer. In what seems to have been a desperate attempt to crank the justice system back into the medieval age in which it had slumbered, Alderson asserted: "..this plea of madness is a palliative of unruly passions leading to murder and is therefore dangerous (to the cause of justice)..." (*Regina -v- Crouch*, 1844).

A similar sentiment was uttered by Lord Bramwell in the trial of wife poisoner, William Dove. In *Regina -v- Dove* 1856,

Bramwell asserted that: "..to a man of weak mind and strong animal propensities….. (such as Dove) the knowledge that the law would not punish him would somehow encourage him to repeat the crime"; notwithstanding the fact that Dove was mentally deficient (of weak mind) and would have no idea that what he did was actually wrong. In this case the Home Secretary agreed with Bramwell and a mentally ill Dove was hanged accordingly. Eleven years later a "feeble-minded" Sophia Usher would be spared.

The essence of the criteria applying in the M'Naghten Rules was: "…that the accused was suffering from (or labouring under) such defect of reason…..and of such disease of the mind… that the accused did not know the nature of his acts or the consequences thereof…" In Frances Kidder's case her counsel, Channell, did not have the time to accumulate sufficient evidence to run the M'Naghten defence and, in any respect, it is doubtful if Justice Byles would have allowed "M'Naghten" in view of the overwhelming evidence given by the stream of witnesses attesting to Frances's cruel treatment of Louisa before and after the accident in July 1867. In other words, it was considered that Frances must have been fully aware of the cruel treatment she was inflicting upon Louisa and there was no possibility of "disease of mind" or "defect of reason" in her case although, as we have seen, newspaper reports and witness testimonies suggest there was clearly something wrong with her mental condition before and after Louisa's murder.

The testimony of Mary Burwell, the Hythe neighbour who came to nurse and help Frances after the accident, was probably the most deadly evidence given at the trial. By the very nature of the woman, who had been a good neighbour in nursing Frances back to health, the jury would have immediately formed a mind-set that she was an honest person who had no cause or reason to vindictively lie, and when Mary had told the court that she had seen Frances: "…throw the child from one room to another…….. which left a lump on her head the size of an egg…", any further testimony may well have been unnecessary in the minds of the jury members. However, when Mary further testified that she had seen Louisa's pinafore "covered in blood", after hearing her receive another beating delivered by Frances upon the poor, defenceless girl, the fate of Frances Kidder was surely sealed. It is, of course, worth noting that much of the "evidence" given at the trial would have been considered inadmissible as hearsay in a modern court. Moreover, it is hoped that, in a modern Britain, Louisa would have been brought to the attention of Social Services long before Frances could inflict further misery upon her, although recent tragic cases may suggest otherwise. Mary Burwell died in late September of 1870. She was 56.

The opportunity to wrest Louisa from her fate was missed after the Kidders' neighbour, William Henniker, took the child to the authorities who then prosecuted Frances at Hythe Magistrates Court where she was fined. In nineteenth century Britain this was clearly not enough and there appears to have been no additional action taken by the authorities; the good neighbour, Henniker, seems to have moved away – to nearby Dymchurch Road – not long after the incident, and after Frances had ruined his trousers. However, the circumstances under which Louisa died were not in dispute and in view of previous comments by Frances to neighbours and friends about her "hatred" of Louisa, together with the attested treatment of the helpless child, the jury were left in no doubt that Frances "wilfully" murdered Louisa and returned a verdict of guilty – with no recommendation for mercy.

From the descriptions of Frances's conduct and behaviour she was either possessed of the most evil of dispositions or she was suffering from a psychological condition: in our modern age, this may be termed as "bipolar"; otherwise known as a manic depressive disorder. A brief investigation into the symptoms of various mental disorders will provide any number of psychological illnesses that could have applied to Frances. But from what we know of her character, together with the manner in which she coldly murdered Louisa, it does not require the considered opinion of an expert in mental illnesses to arrive at the conclusion that there was almost certainly something seriously wrong with Frances and, that being the case, would she have succeeded in a M'Naghten Defence? Given the reports of the continuing "fits", it is self-evident that Frances's mental state was not normal and if these fits or seizures were not apparent before the accident in July of 1867 could they have been caused by a serious head injury such as a fractured skull? There is also the possibility that Frances may have been unwittingly suffering from some other condition that mainly affected females, such as thyroid problems or the condition known to modern medicine as PMT – premenstrual tension – a medical and psychological illness that would not be recognised as an acceptable defence for serious crimes until the 1980s. But in 1868 such a proposition would have been treated with scorn, even though post-natal depression, or a similar condition, seems to have been understood in the case of Sophia Usher.

When Frances Kidder stood trial, the criminal justice system of the nineteenth century was still attempting to come to terms with the M'Naghten Defence and it was, at first, applied sparingly and only to those who were clearly mad when they committed the crime of murder. Many judges shared the view of Lord Alderson, as previously mentioned, and were reluctant to allow 'M'Naghten' because of either public outrage directed at the murderer, who had committed a particularly foul crime, or because the accused was simply "not mad enough". This may have applied to Frances, who displayed what was clearly a dreadful and spiteful temper towards anyone she disliked, but who may not have fulfilled the required criteria of: "......suffering such disease of the mind....that she did not know the nature of her acts or the consequences thereof..." Unlike the tragic Sophia Usher, who was "not bad or mad but sad", Frances Kidder was simply "bad", even though she may also have been "mad". We do not know what attitude Justice Byles adopted in regards to

M'Naghten but, in any respect, it was too late for Mr Channell to formulate a proper defence for Frances who seems to have been left to fend for herself by her husband and her family. In the case of the Turners, perhaps it was understandable that they were unable to provide a legal representation as John Turner's wages were required to feed and clothe what was a large family, even by the standards of the nineteenth century, and this must have taken priority. Moreover, it will appear obvious that John and Frances Turner had resigned themselves to losing their eldest daughter to the gallows; they had ably assisted in sending her there after all.

Since 1836 (with the passing of the Prisoners' Counsel Act) some form of legal representation had to be provided in court for those accused of a capital crime such as wilful murder; hence Justice Byles's appointment of W F Channell for Frances Kidder. Although this could be a lottery regarding the quality and experience of the appointed counsel it did, at the very least, give the accused – or the appointed counsel – an opportunity to question the depositions made by the witnesses or the accusers in the case. Further, at the time of Frances Kidder's trial, legal representation for those who did not have the financial means to defend themselves in the criminal courts was sometimes provided at the discretion of those who administered assistance under the Poor Laws and local charitable trusts. But in Frances's case, the authorities would have risked severe criticism and public admonishment if they had helped a child killer. In the 1860s the average 'consultation fee' of a provincial solicitor was anything from two to five shillings and a defendant could be represented at court for one guinea (£1.05). Another factor may have been that no local solicitor would want to represent or defend a woman who had committed what most people, including the legal profession, saw as an indefensible act against an innocent child: it could have been very bad for business for a local solicitor to take the case. A fee of one guinea was more than a week's wages for William and as he did not even apply for or arrange any legal representation for his wife perhaps he, like her family, had resigned himself to her seemingly inevitable end and he was not the sort of man to throw good money after bad. However, William's inability or reluctance to pay for any kind of legal representation for Frances did not square with the apparent alacrity with which he had paid court costs of £1.2 shillings (£1.10) for Frances's failed summons against their long-suffering neighbours, the Hennikers, in July of 1866.

By the time Frances Kidder had been remanded in custody most, if not all, people – certainly in New Romney and Hythe – regarded her as a cruel and vicious woman who deserved to receive the ultimate punishment. Any sympathy she may have engendered was very thin on the ground, if such sympathy existed at all, and her right to a fair trial, including proper and competent legal representation, was not a priority as far as the outraged citizens of Kent were concerned. In our modern age Frances would have been afforded legal aid and the services of an experienced criminal solicitor and barrister. It is quite possible, once her mental illness had been confirmed, that she would have been charged with – and convicted of – manslaughter, subject to the "Diminished Responsibility" rule, and she would have been "treated" in an institution such as Broadmoor during an indefinite sentence. Even if she had been tried and convicted of murder and not manslaughter, it is possible that she would have served no more than ten years in our current penal system.

Chapter 12

The final days

Frances was now the incumbent of the condemned cell at Maidstone Gaol[2] which, in 1868, was only a few yards from the main gate where her gallows would be erected on the day before she was due to suffer death as prescribed by law. In view of the proximity of the condemned cell to the main gate in County Road, Frances would have heard the sawing and hammering of the dreadful construction, on the eve of her execution, as she walked within the prison grounds with the Reverend Fraser, the last and only person in her life that she could call a friend. Reportedly, workmen began to erect the scaffold on the morning of Wednesday, the 1st of April, and had completed their ghoulish labour at around 11 am on the morning of the execution.

Appeals for the death sentence to be commuted were unsuccessful. There was no appeal procedure in the nineteenth century; the Court of Criminal Appeal would not be established in England until 1907. An insipid and usually ineffectual appeal mechanism was available from the Court for Crown Cases Reserved, established in 1848, amid much criticism from the judiciary. But this was nothing more than a vehicle for discretionary comments from the original trial judge if he thought a point of law could be argued; there was no right of retrial. Justice Byles responded to the appeals by stating, correctly, that under the existing law he could see no reason to amend the sentence or recommend a commutation because he "....could not see any mitigating circumstances in the case", therefore Frances Kidder's only hope was a Royal Pardon, via the Home Secretary, which had been successful in the case of Sophia Usher. But petitions from the "principal inhabitants of Hythe", which included the Mayor, and letters written to the Home Office by the Mayor of New Romney – Mr W D Walker, who had conducted the Inquest and Frances's committal proceedings – and the Reverend Smith, the vicar of New Romney, all fell on deaf ears. Why the Mayors of Hythe and New Romney had risked their considerable reputations in asking for a commutation of sentence for a hated, child-murderess and a neighbourhood nuisance is difficult to understand, but the petitions and pleas for a commutation were based on the assertion that Frances had been ill-treated by her husband and "ill-trained" by her parents; this somewhat enlightened and progressive theme would have sat well in a twenty-first century offender understanding-and-rehabilitation culture, but this was mid-nineteenth century England.

Clearly, the pleas for a commutation of the death sentence were because public opinion began to change as Frances's execution date approached. Although the majority remained steadfast in their view that Frances Kidder should suffer the extreme penalty for her foul deed, a growing number felt that she had somehow been the victim of wretched circumstances and misfortune and that these unfortunate circumstances had somehow made her inflict unrelenting cruelty and a dreadful murder on little Louisa. Reports appeared in the local press of "rumblings among officials in Maidstone Gaol" that if William had been able to provide his wife with legal representation she may have been spared the noose. There were also reports that several members of the jury had begun to express reservations about their verdict because they had not been provided with details of alleged "long ill-treatment" suffered by Frances by her husband. Reportedly, three jury members publicly stated that, had this evidence been presented at the trial, "….a recommendation to mercy at least would have been appended (to the verdict)". But it was too late to apply the brakes to a cycle of events that had been initiated on the evening of the 25th of August 1867, when a defenceless and innocent young girl had been drowned by a wicked and hateful step-mother. And it is difficult to accept that, even if Frances had been afforded a remarkably successful counsel to plead her case, she would not be taking her final steps towards the gallows and whatever kind of eternity awaited her.

In February of 1868, Benjamin Disraeli had succeeded Edward Smith-Stanley (14th Earl of Derby) as Prime Minister; Derby had succumbed to an illness that would kill him in October 1869. In March of 1868 the Home Secretary was a blunt, no-nonsense Bradford born Yorkshireman, Gathorne Hardy, who had no desire to upset was what a sensitive political balance between Disraeli's Conservatives and Gladstone's popular Liberals. A year before parliament had introduced the (New) Reform Act of 1867 (known as the Second Reform Act or Representation of the People Act, 1867), which had given the vote to most male householders and had greatly increased the number of those permitted to vote in a general election. Disraeli thought this legislation would return the Conservatives to office on a wave of public gratitude. He was wrong: Gladstone won the election for the Liberals on the 7th of December that year. But in early 1868 Home Secretary Hardy had his hands full with a crime wave in some of the larger industrial cities and the increasing problems in Ireland, which included a rising Fenian threat in Dublin and London: Fenian bomber Michael Barrett was awaiting execution after being convicted of successfully blowing up Clerkenwell Prison in an attempt to free another Fenian activist, Richard O'Sullivan-Burke. Unfortunately Barrett had also succeeded in demolishing a row of houses, killing 12 people and injuring over 50 others in the process. With a reputation to maintain for being tough on crime, and not wishing to provide ammunition to the Liberals, Hardy was not minded to listen to pleas of clemency for a woman who had become a figure of national hatred as the result of her dreadful crime and trial being reported in the national press: as with many holders of his office, Hardy considered it an act of political suicide to reprieve an evil child killer such as Frances Kidder. The commutation of Sophia Usher's death sentence had been only on the recommendation of the trial judge, not as the result of pleas from members of the public.

Reportedly, Frances confessed her guilt to Reverend Fraser during one of his many visits to her in the condemned cell. She had been fervently reading the Bible and had believed that the Lord would admit her to Heaven if she confessed before dying. The frequency of her "fits" increased and she had to be restrained by the prison warders as she attempted to bash her head against the cell walls. She was also subject to intermittent bouts of screaming and wailing. Her parents visited her three times, including the Tuesday evening before their daughter was scheduled to die.

To add to her misery – if that was possible – William had entered into a relationship with Frances's 17-year-old sister, Adelaide, who had been looking after baby Emma in Hythe.

During the only visit from William, who brought their child Emma on the same Tuesday as her parents, Frances had screamed hysterically at him over his relationship with Adelaide. As William prepared to leave, she again launched into a shouting and screaming "fit" and had to be restrained by warders and the Reverend Fraser. William begged the Reverend to still his wife's yelling, pleading that he and Emma "had to get away" from the cacophony. Later press reports say that after a short conversation Frances and William "had become reconciled" and that William promised to do his best for their daughter, Emma. We are informed, by the local press, that Frances's last family visitor, on the Wednesday, the eve of her execution, was her sister. It is not known if this was the 12 year-old Rhoda or the 20 year-old Mary, both of whom had given evidence against her, but this would have been unlikely. The unnamed sister may have been 24 year-old Emma, Frances's half-sister and the eldest of the Turners' legitimate children. Alternatively, the visiting sister may even have been the 17-year-old Adelaide, with whom William was now cohabiting, although this is also doubtful: with nothing to lose, Frances might have attempted to kill her too. However, if Adelaide was the visiting sister, this last meeting would have been unbearable for both.

The emotional pain, anguish and mental turmoil this 25 year-old woman must have suffered in her final days on Earth cannot be described adequately here.

William Calcraft – Chief Executioner.

Chapter 13

William Calcraft, Chief Executioner

Two or three days after Frances had received the sentence of death from Justice Byles, a grey-bearded 68-year-old man, with flowing white hair, received a hand-delivered official letter from the Home Office, via the Under-Sheriff of Kent, requesting his attendance at Maidstone Gaol no later than the forenoon of Thursday, the 2nd of April 1868.

William Calcraft had been the chief hangman since the 4th April 1829, when he had succeeded John Foxton (sometimes known as 'Foxon'), a psychologically disturbed alcoholic who had held the office since 1820. Born at Little Baddow near Chelmsford in 1800, Calcraft had been a shoemaker by trade and later a butler to a gentleman in Greenwich. He had met Foxton by chance in London and, after expressing an interest in the grisly vocation, and after receiving no more than a brief "training" from Foxton, he had officiated at Lincoln in April of 1829 when he had hanged two men: burglar, Thomas Lister, and highwayman, George Wingfield.

When Foxton died in February or March of 1829, William Calcraft was appointed in April as his successor. The Official Executioner was paid one guinea (21 shillings or £1.05) as a weekly salary and an extra guinea for every execution in London. He was also paid half-a-crown (12.5p) for every flogging required. However, Calcraft was permitted to officiate elsewhere in the country and, as his reputation and experience increased, he often charged as much as ten guineas for a particularly notorious murderer.

Unfortunately for his "clients" the mode of execution employed by Calcraft was years away from the "fracture-dislocation" (of the second and third vertebrae) method where the noosed culprit was rendered instantly unconscious. Calcraft used the "short-drop", which usually resulted in slow strangulation of the prisoner who was left to dangle in agony until Calcraft deigned to pull on the legs to end the suffering. It is an uncomfortable fact that the reason for the placing of the white linen hood over a condemned person's face was not to offer any special dignity to that person who was about to be plunged into oblivion, but moreover to hide the awful spectacle of a face reddening with asphyxiation and of a tongue dropping out of the mouth, and not least to hide from public view the bulging, staring eyes of a person slowly choking to death.

Calcraft's first victim, after he was appointed Chief Executioner, was the notoriously evil 61-year-old governess Esther Hibner who had starved and tortured to death a young female apprentice in her care. On the 13th of April 1829, on the public scaffold at Newgate Jail, now the site of the Old Bailey, Ms Hibner was carried screaming to the gallows, after an attempted suicide, and appeared to have expired soon after Calcraft had released the trapdoor bolts. Sadly, others were not so fortunate. On New Year's Eve 1829, at Newgate, Calcraft hanged Thomas Maynard, the last person to be executed for forgery. After several attempts to adjust the noose, Calcraft made such a botch of it that hardened prison warders turned away in disgust, several attending witnesses fainted, and a large crowd was hushed into silence at the sight and sounds of the 36-year-old hitherto inoffensive Custom House clerk struggling and gasping for over ten minutes at the end of a "short" rope.

Rumours persisted that Calcraft decided which way an offender would die, depending on the gravity of the offence. However, it was well known that this pigeon and rabbit keeper, who often wept when one of his pets died, harboured a particular dislike of child-killers and poisoners. In studying the many nineteenth century death sentences where Calcraft was the executioner, it is not difficult to be persuaded that this servant of the Crown was not only intentionally cruel but that he was also a sadist and probably a sexual deviant. Thomas Hardy illustrates the latter point when he described the effect the execution of Elizabeth Martha Browne had on him when, as a 16-year-old boy, he saw her hanged by Calcraft at Dorchester Prison on Saturday, the 9th of August 1856 for the murder of her younger husband:

".....what a fine figure she showed against the sky as she hung in the rain, and how the tight black silk gown set off her shape as she wheeled half round and back."

The hanging of Elizabeth had a lasting impression on Hardy, which endured until well into his old age. Many commentators have interpreted Hardy's apparent obsession as an erotic experience, which imprinted on his mind when he was a sexually

The execution of Elizabeth Martha Brown at Dorchester prison, which was witnessed by a young Thomas Hardy.

developing adolescent. It is said that Elizabeth and her execution were the inspiration for *"Tess Of The D'Urbervilles"*.

Charles Dickens also witnessed several executions and described them as: *"the fascination of the repulsive, something most of us have experienced"*.

The famous American hangman of the late nineteenth century, George Maledon, was known as "The Prince of Hangmen" and he was originally the chief executioner of American Civil War judge, Isaac "The Hanging Judge" Parker, at Fort Smith in Arkansas. Maledon used the "cowboy knot", which entailed having several loops, similar to the noose that hanged Iraqi leader Saddam Hussein. Maledon's "clients" suffered very little, if at all, and many reports suggest they died instantly, due to the absence of any attested struggle or "twitching". Maledon deployed a "drop" of the length of the man's height – plus two feet – in order to snap the neck at the first four vertebrae, the knot being placed under or next to the left jaw. Maledon's ropes were made – from Manila hemp – exclusively for him in St Louis and he reportedly received what was then an enormous sum of $100 (one hundred dollars) for each execution, such was the regard for his expertise.

Although Calcraft would probably not have been aware of George Maledon and his methods, it is difficult to comprehend why he had not discovered a more efficient and humane science – as Maledon had done – of despatching his charges throughout a career that spanned forty-five years. Calcraft claimed to have introduced the method of pinioning, which included the leather waist belt and wrist straps, so why he could not have 'invented' a humane method of extinguishing life is a mystery. Considering also that, after an all too familiar gruesome execution, he attracted withering scorn, official disapproval and vociferous opprobrium from an outraged public, the press, and several leading politicians, it has to be assumed that Calcraft obtained a degree of pleasure from the pain and torture he surely knew he was inflicting upon those whose last moments were in his hands. And as his advancing years and the strain of his vocation began to take their toll, his incompetence increased. A description of Calcraft by a witness to an execution outside Newgate in 1864 is most appropriate: *"Presently an old and decrepit man arrived and tested the drop......a yell of execration saluted him. This was Calcraft, the hangman, hoary-headed, tottering, and utterly past his usefulness for the work."* (Excerpt from: *Victorian London – Prisons and Penal Systems*: Shire Books – originally published in *Fraser's Magazine*, 1864)

Towards the end of his tenure as chief executioner one of Calcraft's harshest critics was William Marwood, who eventually succeeded him. Reportedly, Marwood had heard of the "fracture-dislocation" method being suggested by surgeons in Dublin who had theorised that such a fracture – and displacement of the spinal cord – would produce "instantaneous" unconsciousness. After conducting various tests on animals Marwood, a Lincolnshire man who, like Calcraft, was a shoemaker by trade, was permitted to perform his first execution at Lincoln Prison, as Calcraft had done. Marwood's debut for his fracture-dislocation occurred on the 1st of April 1872 when he hanged wife-killer William Horry, a man who was completely oblivious to the fact that he was, quite literally, going to go down in history as the first man to be put to death by a new and hitherto untested science. However all was well because, by all accounts, the execution was "successful" as Horry's body was reported to have been "completely still" immediately after he had plunged through the trapdoor with a drop of nearly six feet and with a smaller knot placed under his left jaw.

Following his initial success Marwood mounted a campaign to land the job of chief hangman by coining the phrase: "Calcraft chokes them, I execute them". After receiving positive reports about Horry's execution and several others, a relieved Home Office appointed Marwood in 1874 to replace the retiring and increasingly bungling Calcraft, whose recent executions – according to prison staff, doctors and news reporters – had been nothing short of garrottings. Soon after his appointment as chief executioner the children of Whitechapel, in the east end of London, often ran through the grimy, rat-infested streets chanting: "If pa killed ma, who would kill pa? – Marwood!"

The fracture-dislocation method of judicial execution was finally perfected by hangmen Berry, Billington, and the Pierrepoint family (Henry and his brother Thomas) at the end of the nineteenth century, and was turned into an art form by Henry's famous son, Albert, who succeeded his uncle Thomas around 1940. Albert's first hanging as chief executioner was that of gangster Tony Mancini at Pentonville on the 17th of October, 1941. Reportedly, Mancini shouted "cheerio, everybody" just before the trapdoor was sprung. At Albert's hands he died instantly.

Regrettably the quest for the ideal and publicly acceptable judicial killing suffered the occasional setback, which included an unfortunate occurrence at the execution of Robert Goodale at Norwich Castle, on the 30th of November 1885, when ex-Yorkshire policeman James Berry was the hangman. At just over fifteen stone Goodale was considered obese, compared to the average weight for the late nineteenth century, and Berry had calculated a drop of 5 feet 9 inches. His book of 'drop' calculations, compiled after several years of painstaking comments and notes, suggested a drop of 7 feet 6 inches, but Berry had considered this too long and could have resulted in "complications", in view of Goodale's weight. Sadly, his calculations were in serious error because, immediately after the trapdoors had crashed down, Berry and the assembled witnesses, including the prison chaplain, stood in horror on the scaffold as they saw the rope bounce back up without Goodale on the end of it. When they looked into the pit they saw the dreadful sight of Goodale's body several feet from his hooded head. Doubtless Mr Berry hastily revised his "weight and drop" calculations after this abomination but there was another regrettable event at Kirkdale Prison in 1892 when, again, the condemned man was almost decapitated. On this occasion he blamed the prison medical officer for interference in his suggested length of drop, but that same year Mr Berry was relieved of his duties by a nervous Home Office.

The luckless Berry was also the executioner on the renowned occasion at Exeter Prison, on February 23rd 1885, when he made three attempts to execute 19-year-old murderer, John "The Man They Couldn't Hang" Lee. After the third failure – when the trapdoor lever had been pulled but a strapped and hooded Lee still stood patiently and unmoving on the scaffold – a thoroughly distraught prison governor ordered Lee to be returned to his cell. Thereafter Home Secretary, Sir William Harcourt, commuted the sentence to life imprisonment. It was reported that, upon returning to his cell, Lee had been offered and had gratefully wolfed down his executioner's breakfast after a speechless and thoroughly bewildered Berry had refused the meal. A few weeks later, an official report stated that an incorrectly installed gallows mechanism had allowed the trapdoor bolts to rest on the drawbar, thus preventing them from opening when weight was placed upon them. It was also suggested that Divine Intervention may have been responsible because, it was later discovered, when the prison chaplain had stood on the scaffold floorboard his weight may have increased the pressure on the faulty trapdoor bolts. Lee successfully petitioned for his freedom and was finally released in 1907. He died in 1945 at the very respectable age of 81.

Calcraft's last job was the hanging of James Godwin, on the 25th of May 1874, at Newgate, when he botched that too: it was reported that Godwin's white linen hood was seen "being sucked in" until his expiry several minutes after he had dropped just four feet. William Calcraft received a retirement pension of £1 and 5 shillings (£1.25) per week from the Home Office until he died at his home in Hoxton, London on the 13th December 1879.

It was perhaps fortunate, therefore, that Frances Kidder had not been acquainted with the gallows lore relating to her deliverer unto the hereafter as she prayed with the Reverend Fraser in her condemned cell in the early morning of her last day on Earth.

Chapter 14

The execution of Frances Kidder – 12 noon, Thursday 2nd April 1868

On the morning of Friday the 27th of March 1868, the governor of Maidstone Gaol, Major Bannister, accompanied by Reverend Fraser, went to the condemned cell to read Frances's death warrant to her. We are informed that she "manifested no signs of emotion whatever on this being read" *(Kentish Express)* but not long after, Frances had wept and wailed frequently. From this day to the morning of her execution, the Reverend Fraser would visit Frances regularly, sometimes three times a day, to pray with her and to offer spiritual strength; there was now nothing more for Frances Kidder to receive.

Maidstone Gaol was built between the years 1811 and 1818 and from 1831 the jail was the normal place of execution for those sentenced to death in the county of Kent. Before this time the condemned were hanged at the crossroads at Penenden Heath (now a mini-roundabout) where they were "turned off" a ladder or a cart and left to dangle accordingly. William Calcraft carried out the last executions of this type on the Heath on Christmas Eve 1830, when he hanged three men for arson.

For the execution of Frances Kidder the gallows that had been used to hang 29-year-old Ann Lawrence the previous year had been re-erected outside the main gate of the prison and in full public view, however a black cloth was draped over the bottom of the gallows so that only the top half of the condemned could be seen.

Ann Lawrence had murdered her young son, Jesse, in Tunbridge Wells on 14th April 1866. At noon on Thursday the 10th of January 1867, she was hanged, along with another prisoner, 20-year-old James Fletcher, a Derbyshire miner who had murdered a warden at Chatham Prison. Mr Calcraft had officiated and, it was reported, the rough-and-ready young miner – who, one supposes, had nothing to lose – called the man who was to launch him into oblivion a particularly offensive name before the white hood was placed over his head. Ironically, at her trial on the 20th of December 1866, Ann had been sentenced to death by judge W F Channell, the man who would appear as defence counsel for Frances just over a year later.

Maidstone always hanged at noon and for the execution of Frances Kidder on that bright, spring morning, a large crowd – estimates suggest over 2,000 – had gathered in front of the gaol in Court Road (opposite the row of little terraced houses of Camden Street) to witness what would be the last public hanging in England of a woman.

To entertain the assembled right-thinking members of society, anxious to see justice administered in their name, jugglers, tumblers, and "masters of magick" performed their time-honoured routines for a few pennies that were thrown into crumpled hats, and piemen sold pasties and savouries to anyone who could muster an appetite. Frequently, at public executions, fake pamphlets or "broadsides" quoting "The Final Death Cell Confessions" of the condemned were sold at a few pennies each. But Frances Kidder had spoken – and, apparently confessed – only to the good Reverend Fraser.

Reportedly, Frances had "slept a few hours" and had enjoyed her breakfast. Thereafter, she had done little else but pray with

Reverend Fraser, reciting "Jesu, my Saviour" endlessly. She received letters from William and her parents, which were read to her. William's letter – probably written for him – began: "To my darling wife..." and had ended with: "... if you had taken my advice, this would not have occurred...": not for the first time would the phrase involving the words "horse" and "bolted" apply to Mr William Kidder.

As noon approached, there was a flurry of activity and several officials appeared at the main gate of the prison and the gallows as if to signal a commencement of the proceedings. Inside the prison, and a short walk to the main gate, Ashford solicitor, Robert Furley, the Under Sheriff of Kent, together with several wardens, all followed Calcraft to the condemned cell where a pale, weak and penitent Frances was praying fervently with the Reverend Fraser; one newspaper reported that she became "hysterical" upon the appearance of Calcraft and his straps.

Working with a well-honed routine, and with a quick smile of rotting teeth through his silver-grey beard, a silent Calcraft pinioned (tied) Frances's hands together and escorted her from the condemned cell. The Reverend Fraser held a pinioned hand as she was led out across the yard to the main gate, which opened to reveal before her the gallows and the last steps she would take in this lifetime. With the Reverend following, two warders gently helped Frances up the steps and onto the platform where she and Reverend Fraser began to whisper prayers. After positioning her on the trapdoors, Calcraft pinioned her arms by wrapping a leather strap around her body at the elbows. The Chief Executioner then bound Frances's legs over her dress with a thin leather strap and reached to adjust the chain, which was attached to the smooth hemp rope (execution ropes were produced by John Edgington & Co in The Old Kent Road and Bridport Gundry in Dorset). Just before Calcraft placed the white cap over her head and the noose around her neck, Frances looked at Reverend Fraser and smiled a thank you. Then, as the stiff linen bag eclipsed her last view of life, she reportedly cried out: "Oh Lord, oh Lord Jesu forgive me" and the assembled crowd were stilled in silence.

Suddenly, there was a loud bang and 25-year-old Frances Kidder dropped just a few feet, which meant that a merciful death would not come swiftly to a body that had now begun to writhe in slow strangulation; a body that was dressed in the clothes Frances had put on in her parents' bedroom soon after she had murdered little Louisa just over six months before.

There were no raucous, righteous cheers; no hollering or jeering that this vile murderess had got her just deserts; just a heavy, sustained silence as the gathering saw the top half of the young hooded body, violently twisting in agony for nearly three minutes. Then all was still and life had finally left Frances Kidder, born on the 4th of November 1842, the illegitimate daughter of John Vousden and Frances Drury in the parish of Brenchley in Kent, and the mother of a young daughter. Justice had been seen to be done and the crowd, many young women from Hythe and New Romney among them, melted away like an ebbing tide, their heads bowed in grief.

Aftermath

After Frances had been buried in an unmarked grave within the prison grounds there was some sympathy for her in the press and from the public, many of whom had previously expressed their disgust at the fate of young Louisa and who had called for Frances to be hanged from the nearest tree. Many newspapers, including *The Times* and *The Telegraph*, after months of unremitting condemnation of Frances, turned their wrath on William Kidder and how he had treated his wife; how he had deserted her in prison and taken up with her younger sister and why had he not provided her with proper legal representation. It was also reported that a hanging effigy of him was burned in Hythe after the execution and bricks and other large objects were thrown at his house. One newspaper reported that William watched his wife hang and had then sped off on his pony and cart after being recognised and pursued by an angry mob, although this was not reported in any other journal.

However we learn from local newspaper reports that, on the night of the execution, William Henniker, the next door neighbour who had reported Frances to Hythe magistrates in 1866, and a local chimney sweep, David Weeks, were arrested and summonsed for malicious damage and accused of throwing tiles and other objects at William's house in Theatre Street in which he appears to have been living permanently with Adelaide, Frances's 17-year-old sister. Indeed, Adelaide gives evidence against the two accused in the magistrates court but the case is thrown out, after which: "...the large number of persons assembled in the court applauded lustily". As we have seen, Mr Henniker had moved away from his troublesome neighbours in 1866 and he also had an 'altercation' with an unfortunate Mr Middleton in the Dymchurch Road in June of 1867, so he had a propensity for violent actions and this seems to have been another manifestation of his unforgiving nature; what advantage he could possibly have achieved by throwing objects at the previous home of a woman he clearly hated, but who had died that day in the most appalling manner, is not clear.

Lloyd's Weekly, one of the largest circulated Sunday newspapers of the time, added to the opprobrium by reporting that William had publicly humiliated Frances in Hythe on many occasions and that he had claimed Louisa was actually Frances's child. The paper also re-iterated and emphasised his cohabiting with Frances's 17-year-old sister before and after the execution.

And in a 'Letter To The Editor' to *The Kentish Express* of Saturday the 4th of April 1868, two days after her execution, Frances had an unexpected apologist in the form of the Under Sheriff of Kent, Mr Robert Furley, the Ashford solicitor who was present on the scaffold. Furley, clearly a righteous man, writes that, although: "... *the laws of God and man have been vindicated......is there no lesson to be learnt?*" Furley goes on to blame John and Frances Turner for being bad parents, who should have done what the Reverend Fraser did (instruct Frances in the Bible), and William for not providing any defence for his wife. The good Furley tells in his letter that New Romney has one of the best national schools in the country and that the vicar of the parish is an "energetic" man who pays great attention to the education of the children of the poor. From Furley's letter we learn that John Turner is seen as an "undesirable" because "he had no regular master"; meaning that he was a self-employed labourer and probably hiring himself out to several employers in the New Romney area. This was not an uncommon employment status in mid-nineteenth century England: farm labourers often worked for whoever paid the best rates and if a man had a particular skill, such as haymaking, harvesting or horse-ploughing, he could take his skill, or speciality, to the employer most likely to pay him the best wage for his efforts; and in the 1860s farm labourers went for any work available. No doubt Mr Furley was an ardent advocate of the Statute of Labourers, enacted by Edward III in 1351, which prevented farm and estate workers from moving to higher paying landowners who had suffered labour shortages as a result of The Black Death. In any respect, the virtuous Furley holds forth in his letter that, had Frances found God in time, she would not have relentlessly tortured and beaten the life out of a helpless and innocent child before drowning her in a ditch.

William seems to have been prepared to ride out the storm of abuse, accusations and notoriety because, in the Census of 1881, he is still registered as living at Theatre Street, Hythe, aged 52, and described as a "general dealer" and 16-year-old Emma is recorded as living with him. However, in Pike's Directory for Hythe of 1887 a William Kidder, "dealer", is living alone in Prospect Place.

The tragic case of Frances and Louisa is littered with strange coincidences. We know that the Reverend Edward Turner, the Rector of Maresfield in Sussex, produced a brief history of the Kidder family in 1850; an unimportant but interesting connection of the two family names. Throughout the mid- to late-eighteenth and early nineteenth centuries, a large amount of land in the New Romney area was owned by the Dering family of Pluckley. A family member, possibly the young Edward Dering, was the assistant prosecutor at Frances's murder trial at Maidstone. The last Tory MP for New Romney, before the constituency was abolished in 1832, was Sir Edward Cholmeley Dering. Benjamin Cobb, of the family of "Mr Cobb's bridge", where Frances drowned Louisa, was the election agent of the Dering family in the early nineteenth century and the Cobb family owned farm and grazing land in the Romney area on which John Turner probably worked as it was near to his home, which was also owned by the Cobb family.

Hothfield was the birthplace of Eliza Staples, the mother of Louisa. Eliza's birthplace, "Hothfield Street", is situated near the road on which Frances would have travelled on her final journey in the prison van to Maidstone Gaol and one wonders if she caught a poignant glimpse of what would have been a small hamlet, surrounded by the woodland and grazing lands of Hothfield Common. And on that morning of the 29th of August 1867, as the prison van trotted over the Common towards the village of Charing and its coaching house, the King's Head, where the horses and Frances would have been refreshed, did she whisper to herself: "Oh Eliza, if only you had lived, I would not be going to my death"?

Frances and William baptised Emma on the 12th of March, 1865: exactly three years later, on the 12th of March 1868, Frances is standing in the dock at Maidstone Assize Court charged with wilful murder. John Turner and Frances Drury are married on the 2nd of April 1843: exactly 25 years later, on the 2nd of April 1868, their daughter is publicly hanged on their Silver Wedding anniversary.

Epilogue

The last public execution in England was carried out by William Calcraft when he hanged Fenian bomber Michael Barrett on Tuesday, the 26th of May 1868 outside Newgate Prison. Amid the booing, jeering, and the singing of "Rule Britannia" by a large crowd, Barrett's body was seen to 'jerk' several times on the rope. On the 29th of May 1868, three days after Barrett had been choked to death in full public view, The Capital Punishment (Within Prisons) Bill passed into law and the botched executions of the capital sentence by an ageing incompetent could be witnessed only by appalled prison governors and staff and the few press reporters allowed in the death chamber; Calcraft's tenure of bungling and sadism had six more years to run, as the unfortunate James Godwin would prove on the 25th of May 1874.

The last public hanging in the British Isles took place in St Helier, Jersey on the 11th of August 1875, when Joseph Philip Le Brun was despatched by William Marwood for the murder of his sister and the attempted murder of his brother-in-law. The Capital Punishment Amendment (Within Prisons) Act 1868 did not apply to the Channel Islands, which finally abolished public executions in 1907.

Almost exactly 89 years after the execution of Le Brun, the last executions in Britain occurred on the morning of the 13th of August 1964 when Peter Anthony Allen was hanged at Walton Jail, Liverpool and Gwynne Owen Evans (born John Robson

Walby) was hanged at Strangeways, Manchester for the murder of van driver, John West in Workington on the 7th of April 1964.

The last execution at Maidstone Prison was on the 8th of April 1930, just over 62 years after that of Frances Kidder, when 31-year-old Sidney Fox was hanged for the murder of his doting mother at a Margate hotel on the 22nd of October 1929, after a trial at Lewes Assizes. Fox was despatched by hangman Robert Baxter from Hertford who, in 1927, was severely reprimanded along with Thomas Pierrepoint, Albert's uncle, after being discovered "touting" for business from county under-sheriffs. Not long after Fox's execution, the condemned cell and gallows were dismantled; the old condemned cell is now in the prison reception area.

The last woman to hang for capital murder in the British Isles was Ruth Ellis (nee Hornby) who was executed by Albert Pierrepoint at Holloway Prison on Wednesday, the 13th July 1955 at 9am. Ruth Ellis had pumped four bullets from a Smith & Wesson.38 service revolver into her lover David Blakely outside the *Magdala* public house in Tanza Road, Hampstead on Easter Monday, 1955. As a consequence of the Ruth Ellis case, the 'defence' of Diminished Responsibility was placed on the statute book in 1957.

Although we know little of William Kidder and what kind of a man he was, his conduct after his wife's sentence of death, together with his subsequent behaviour with her younger sister, the 17-year-old Adelaide, says a lot about the character and attitude of the man. However, in what may have been either an unfortunate coincidence, or an illustration of William's arrogance, is that next to a report of his wife's execution, in *The Kentish Express* of the 4th of April 1868, there is an advertisement, placed by William, for the sale of 40 sacks of potatoes. It may be another coincidence that this appears to be William Kidder's only advertisement in the *Kentish Express* for the year of 1868.

In August of that year William appeared in the Hythe County Court, summonsed by Richard Staples for non-payment of an agreed cost of upkeep for young Ellen. From the report of the case (*Kentish Express* 22nd August 1868) it appears that this is not the first time William has appeared in connection with Ellen's "maintenance". The reported dialogue of the case also provides us with another aspect of William Kidder's attitude and demeanour. The case was heard before a Mr G Wilks, the Registrar and the man who drew up the original agreement between William and Richard Staples confirming William's payment of one shilling and sixpence per week (7.5 new pence) to Richard for Ellen's provision:

Staples: "But you have no proper home for it (Ellen). You told me yourself you had not had a mouthful of victuals there either on Friday or Saturday. What is the use of bringing the child to such a place as that is; you know you have not a wife there (William is living with Frances's 17-year-old sister, Adelaide)."

Kidder: "That does not signify."

Staples: "Indeed it does and while it is so I shall keep you to your agreement to pay me 1s 6d a week as long as I choose to keep the child."

The Registrar: "You have the agreement with you?"

Staples: "I have sir; before his wife was hung he told me it was all her fault but I always had the money then and since I have not been able to get it."

Kidder: "Well, why don't you send the child away?"

Staples: "I should be willing to give the child up if you had a decent home to bring it to. But I will not bring it to Hythe for it to have to run about the streets dirty and neglected or for it to be starved and for people to give it food out of pity as was the case with the other poor thing that was made off with (Louisa)."

Kidder: "Well, I couldn't help that."

The Registrar: "Were you married to the mother?"

Richard Staples interjects: "No he was not, sir; they told us they were married and we did not know different until this child was christened. I went and took my daughter away, and she was half dead then, and she died at my house when the child was three months old. I do not want him to have the child for it to be treated like the other poor thing was."

It appears that Eliza suffered serious post-natal infection or something similar as a consequence of giving birth to Ellen and this was possibly the cause of her death in August of 1863. As Ellen was baptised on the 8th of February 1863 she was probably born not long before, therefore she would have been at least six months old when Eliza died in late August (she was buried in the churchyard of St Mary's, Sellindge on the 28th of August 1863).

The case was adjourned until the return of the County Court judge who gave judgment to Richard accordingly. William was ordered to pay 5 shillings a month to Richard to pay off arrears outstanding of 16 shillings and 6d. Whether or not William honoured the judgment we do not know but in the 1871 Census for Sellindge, 8-year-old Ellen Kidder-Staples is still living with the family. The fact that William was in dire straits is evident; he seems to have been in a similar situation when Richard Staples felt compelled to return "the poor thing" (Louisa) after William had failed to honour the agreement – legal or otherwise – to pay for her upkeep. William also feels no compunction in blaming Frances for Richard not receiving payment for Louisa; in view of what appears to have been an almost perpetual cycle of payments in court fines and fees for Frances's behaviour, he may have had some justification.

What kind of life William led in the years following the execution of his wife we do not know but it could not have been comfortable for him being commonly known as the husband of a child-killer; the name "Kidder" would have resonated with many people in Kent, especially in Hythe and New Romney. There would also have been the lingering doubts in the minds of many, and certainly of those who knew him, that he could have prevented the terrible treatment suffered by Louisa and that he could easily have protected her from Frances's "ungovernable fury". There is no record of him marrying Adelaide – a girl 23 years his junior – or anyone else. He moved from Prospect Place to Market Street (later Dymchurch Road) after 1901 and lived alone until his death in late June 1908 at the age of nearly 80 years. He was buried on the 4th of July 1908.

On the 13th of August 1891 Emma Kidder married Benjamin Thomas Jones, a "groom" at the Hythe Barracks, in the parish church of St Leonard's where her parents were wed on the 1st of February 1865. On the marriage certificate Benjamin's age is given as 25 but Emma seems to have succumbed to vanity by recording her age as "24", when in fact she is 26 and will be 27 on the 26th of December 1891: a similar "error" was made by her father in February 1865. The service was conducted by H E Sawyer and the witnesses were a William Vicksage and his wife, Eugenie. William Kidder is mentioned on the marriage certificate but if he did give Emma away to Benjamin, one wonders if his mind recalled that day in August 1867 when he gave his wife Frances to another Benjamin: Constable Aspinall of New Romney police station.

In the 1911 Census, where Benjamin is recorded as aged 44 and Emma as aged 45, they are shown as living in William's last home in Market Street (Dymchurch Road), Hythe. There is no record of any children by the couple and Benjamin predeceased Emma by ten years. Emma continued to live in the house on her own until her death, in a Hastings hospital, on the 2nd of November 1949. She is recorded as being 84 years at the time of her burial – in Hythe on the 8th of November, 1949 – but she was nearly a year older, having been born on the 26th of December 1864.

Three years after his adopted daughter was publicly hanged John Turner died, aged 54, and was buried in New Romney (St Nicholas's Church) on the 21st of June 1871. The Reverend Robert Smith, who had pleaded for a commutation of Frances's death sentence, officiated. Normal life for John and Frances Turner effectively ended on that dreadful night of the 25th of August 1867, when they handed over their daughter to the law of the land knowing, as they surely must have, what the consequences would be; forever they would be known and condemned as the parents of a child killer. In 1871 the average male life span was considered to be aged 45, so 54 years was a comparatively old age. But John Turner must have been a fit man, having laboured most of his adult life in the fresh air, and one wonders what the cause of his death was; his heart must have been broken by the events of August 1867 to April 1868. It is not difficult to imagine what thoughts Frances Turner would have had seeing her firstborn child for the last time in the dark and dingy citadel that was Maidstone Gaol where her dysfunctional life would end, and we can only speculate on how she coped with being the true mother of an evil murderess. And on the morning of the 2nd of April 1868 would a 43 year-old John Vousden have known that his illegitimate child was about to make history as the last woman to be hanged in public?

And for poor little Louisa, whose short life was tragically ended after two and a half years of unremitting cruelty: may she forever rest in peace.

Notes

(1) The Biron family was of Irish descent and owned substantial lands and property in Rosscommon and elsewhere in Ireland. The family also owned property in England, including homes in Norfolk Square, Paddington, London, Lympne, Maidstone, and Eastbourne. The father of prosecution counsel, Robert John Biron, was the Reverend Edwin Biron, the vicar of Lympne from 1840 until his death in 1870, and also chairman of the Kent County Petty Sessions in 1868. Robert's brother, Henry Brydges Biron, was a Kent county cricketer. The family seems to have been associated with the "Irish problem", which is hardly surprising considering their influence, wealth and landed possessions in the troubled isle. The Reverend Biron was a convert to Roman Catholicism at a time when the Fenian (later IRA) movement in Ireland was gaining ground and when there was a great deal of Irish fervour and sympathy for the Irish in British politics, particularly as a result of the potato famine of the 1840s and 1850s. Catholics were given the right to vote in 1829 and in the mid-nineteenth century The Oxford Movement was formed by Catholic-sympathising academics and the Reverend Biron seems to have allied himself to this cause. The Movement was given impetus by the conversion of many leading Anglican church figures, including John Henry Newman – later Cardinal Newman – who converted to Catholicism in 1845.

Robert Biron, Cambridge University MA and a member of Lincoln's Inn, was a leading prosecutor in Kent and later in London. He was also a Recorder of Hythe. Robert married Jane, the sister of eminent QC Frederick Andrew Inderwick. Their son, Chartres Biron, born in 1863, became a prominent lawyer and judge and was knighted in 1920. In November of 1928 Sir Chartres, as Chief Magistrate at Old Street Magistrates Court, was involved in one of the most controversial trials of the age when he ordered the novel *"The Well Of Loneliness"*, by lesbian author Radclyffe Hall, to be destroyed on the grounds that it was "obscene". (At this time, the term applied to lesbians was "sexual inverts".) An Appeal, held at the London Quarter Sessions, was dismissed after only five minutes.

In early October 1894, Jane Biron visited the studios of celebrated photographer, William Atkinson in Grove Road, Eastbourne to have a photograph taken of her dog. Whilst Atkinson was taking a second plate, Jane suffered a severe stroke from which she did not recover. She died shortly after, aged 55 years. Robert was devastated by her death and, according to colleagues, he was "never the same man (in court) again." Robert's sister, Elizabeth Biron, married Sir James Charles Mathew, later an eminent Lord Chief Justice. Their daughter, also Elizabeth, married John Dillon, the Irish land reform protagonist and Home Rule agitator and last leader of the Irish Reform Party.

(2) For some reason, HM Prison Service press and public relations office could not advise where the old Maidstone Prison condemned cell was, nor could several members of the staff at the prison. However, in correspondence with *The Kent Messenger* in September of 2008, Mr Bernard Dunn, the ex governor of Maidstone Prison, said that the old condemned cell was where the "prison reception area" is now. The reception area, I am informed, is – or was – behind the gate in County Road, in front of which Frances Kidder was hanged.

Acknowledgements

The research for this book entailed hours upon hours of poring over documents and newspaper reports relating to Hythe and New Romney in the mid-1860s. Whilst internet sources were appreciated, it must be said that the majority of the facts, data, and information contained in this book have been acquired through the old-fashioned method of research in the libraries, without whom the book simply would not have been possible. The internet, with its incredible "search engines", proved to be an invaluable tool for accessing knowledge and obtaining information that would otherwise have been unavailable. Unfortunately, an uncomfortable amount of information I obtained from internet sources proved to be inaccurate and conflicting. For example, on one "search for your ancestors" type of website I found 25-year-old Emma Kidder named as the "wife" of 50 year old William Kidder; on another I found New Romney placed in Sussex; and on yet another – when I was doing a "test run" – after correctly entering my own birthplace and date details, I discovered I did not exist.

In an age in which information may be obtained, accessed, and stored with no more effort than a "click", our libraries may seem entirely incompatible and even an anachronism in a brave new world of information technology. But as I discovered time and again it was the libraries, with their vast banks of easily accessible documents, that proved to be indispensable. With the evident collapse of our education system, and the inevitable academic atrophy, we now live in a society that seems to be unavoidably returning to an earlier medieval period of illiteracy and ignorance, when only academics and intellectuals possessed the skills of writing and communication. It is clear, therefore, that we must preserve and even cherish our libraries if our society is to stand any chance of progress from the educational desert in which it currently languishes. It appears that, although we are now possessed of an incredibly advanced technology, we have not developed the concomitant intellectual capacity to benefit from it.

My warm thanks goes to the following libraries and their kind and helpful staff:

Ashford, New Romney, Hythe, Folkestone, Maidstone, and Tunbridge Wells.

My appreciation and thanks also to: Kent County Council at County Hall, especially Stephen. The Public Records Office at Kew (The National Archives). Register of Births, Deaths, & Marriages at Tunbridge Wells, especially Steve. The East Kent Archives. The Centre For Kentish Studies. Maidstone Museum. The Police Museum at Chatham. The Marsh Academy, especially Mervyn. New Romney Town Council, especially The Town Clerk. Shaw, Rabson & Co, Estate Agents, especially Debbie. Shepway District Council. Hothfield History Society, especially Karen. Brenchley and Matfield History Society. Miss D Rayner, Hythe local historian. And many thanks to Paul in New Romney.

Bibliography and References

Local newspapers: *Maidstone Telegraph*; *Maidstone & Kentish Journal*; *South Eastern Gazette*; *Kentish Express & Ashford News*; *Folkestone Express*. National newspapers: *Daily Telegraph*, *The Times*.

Francis Kidder – The Last Woman To Be Hanged In Public, by John Aspin (self-published, 1990/1991) – Clifford Elmer Books, Cheadle, Cheshire SK8 5EQ

True Crimes From The Past – Kent, by W H Johnson, Countryside Books, 2005

The Oxford Illustrated History of Britain, Edited by K. O. Morgan, Oxford University Press 1984

The Hangmen of England, Horace Bleackley, 1929 and later editions.

Census: 1841, 1851, 1861, 1881, 1891.

Local Parish Records: Ashford, Folkestone, Hythe, New Romney, Brenchley.

Electoral Rolls for New Romney and Hythe: 1911 to 1949.

Various "genealogical" websites.

Index